STAYING ALIVE

THE PARATROOPER'S STORY

John Delaney

with Jan Greenough

MONARCH
BOOKS

Oxford, UK and Grand Rapids, Michigan

First published in the UK by Monarch Books
(a publishing imprint of Lion Hudson plc),
Mayfield House, 256 Banbury Road, Oxford OX2 7DH
Tel: +44 (0) 1865 302750 Fax: +44 (0) 1865 302757
Email: monarch@lionhudson.com
www.lionhudson.com

UK ISBN 1 85424 670 4
US ISBN 0 8254 6073 5

Distributed by:
UK: Marston Book Services Ltd, PO Box 269,
Abingdon, Oxon OX14 4YN;
USA: Kregel Publications, PO Box 2607,
Grand Rapids, Michigan 49501.

British Library Cataloguing Data
A catalogue record for this book is available
from the British Library.

Printed and bound in Great Britain by Bookmarque Ltd

Dedication

THIS BOOK IS DEDICATED to my wife and friend, Tara Sarah Elizabeth. Thank you for the love, grace and care you have shown me; for hanging in there, in the good and hard times; for bearing our children; for believing in me; and for walking out this path that we have chosen for our lives.

Contents

Prologue

THE PLANE IS A SECOND-WORLD-WAR Douglas Dakota DC3, nicknamed the ParaDaks. It's circling the airfield at 800 feet, and inside 16 men are waiting to jump. You've trained for this moment. You've stepped out of mock-up planes in the hangar, you've done performance rolls attached to rigging lines, you've jumped off a ramp till your knees were bruised, but that was all make-believe. This is the real thing – your first live jump.

There's a shout: "Stand up! Hook up!" Time to get in line. Check the pin on your static line, check for free movement on the cable. Check the reserve chute, strapped to your front. Turn on the spot – one. Check the chute on the man behind you – two. Tap him on the head so he knows he's OK – three. Turn back to face front.

The dispatchers are waiting at the open door, the noise of the propellers is deafening, and the wind's buffeting the smell of aviation fuel into the plane. "Count down!" The guy at the back slaps the next one on the shoulder: "Sixteen right!" "Fifteen right!" and you count forward from the back. Every shout is rhythmic, every move in perfect timing, because you've trained together so hard you're like a well-oiled machine.

"Action – stations!" shouts the dispatcher. You repeat the order, 16 voices shouting together like one man: "Action – stations!" March to the door in the Para step – one, two, one, two, stomp.

Then you wait. Red light – green light – the hooter sounds, one long blare. "Stand in the door!" The stick of men shout back: "Stand in the door!"

The first guy's in the door, eyes fixed ahead, arm up, one hand holding the strop. "Go!" He throws it aside and he's gone. One, two, stomp, the rest of you move forward. "Go!"

Now it's you. You're at the front by the open doorway, prop wash in your face, dispatcher each side, and no time to think, no chance to hesitate, because the one, two, stomp and the shouted rhythm of the ParaBats haul you forward. "Go!"

Out and falling, chin down, arms folded across your chest in the compact position, knees bent, feet together. The strop pulls the parachute, and it deploys above you with a sharp tug on your harness. Look up and check you can see the apex of the chute. Check below, look left and right. All clear.

From below it all looks so peaceful – all those canopies billowing open silently and floating down so slowly – but up here your heart's beating fast and you're braced for action, working all the time, checking the landmarks for drift, hauling on your harness to make sure you're coming down into the wind. But still you want to shout with exhilaration as the blood surges through your veins and you feel so alive – you're high on adrenalin and tension.

Now the ground's rushing up towards you and you hit the earth, rolling to absorb the impact and feeling the tug of the collapsing chute. Get up, fast, twist the chute into a string and pull the apex through into a tight bundle with a swift, practised movement. You've done it – your first jump. You want to shout and punch the air, but you grab your gear and move off. Now, at last, you've made it; you've got where you want to be. You're one of the elite – the Parachute Battalion.

CHAPTER ①

Johannesburg Childhood

I ALWAYS KNEW THAT ONE DAY I would be a soldier; every white South African boy knew that. It was what you did when you finished school. I was born in 1962, and conscription was introduced in 1967, so for as long as I could remember, the army had been part of my thinking. All through my life the older boys – including my uncle and brother – finished school at the age of 18 and went into the armed forces. The only decision to be made was whether to do your National Service before or after completing your studies, if you were going on to college. Refusing to join up wasn't an option: the alternative was three years in jail. I never questioned it.

I was born into an ordinary South African family, living in Johannesburg. The Delaneys were white South Africans of Irish extraction; they had emigrated to England in the 1880s and moved from there to South Africa in the early 1900s. I was named John after my grandfather. My mother, on the other hand, was a much more recent immigrant. She grew up in England during the war, and moved to South Africa at the age of fifteen with her parents and her two sisters. Both families were devout Roman Catholics and attended Mass every Sunday; my parents met at a church social.

They married in 1958, and promptly produced four children in five years: my sister Carol, my brother Neil Andrew (always known as Andy), then me, and finally Janice. The other three were all dark-haired, and stood out among the other families in our neighbourhood, who mostly had the distinctive pale Dutch or English looks of white South Africans. I was the odd one out in our family, with blue eyes and blond hair. People often asked my mother where she came from, because of her British accent; if they noticed my hair colour, I used to say, "They bought me from the supermarket on the corner!"

We were a large and close-knit family: my father had a sister nine years younger and a brother who was 17 years younger than him. My uncle Jimmy was more like an older brother to us, because we were so close in age. My grandfather died the year before I was born, but we saw a lot of my grandmother Biddy and my great-grandmother Ouma, and all the various cousins and second cousins who were always visiting their house.

My mother's parents also lived nearby, and we visited them every other Sunday. Granny Frances was a wise and loving person; my mother spent hours talking to her on the phone. She always had time to tell us exciting stories about the Blitz, when the Luftwaffe sent over bombers to destroy the ammunition factories in the north of England: my grandfather Jerry would be on duty as a fire-spotter at night, and she and the three little girls used to hide under the solid-oak dining table for protection. The pair of them loved to spoil us with sweets and our favourite treat, fish and chips from the takeaway. On Sunday evenings I used to follow Grandpa out to the pantry where he kept his stash of Bell's Whisky. Safely hidden from prying eyes, he used to fill his glass to the top and down it in one gulp; then he would put in a small amount more, top it up with water and ice, and take this modest-looking drink back into the living room to join the rest of the unsuspecting family. He would repeat this ritual several times during the evening, and was often swaying noticeably by the time we left.

We lived in a typical South African home, a one-storey house in the suburbs of Johannesburg. My father had trained as an engineer at Wits University, and worked his way up to managerial positions in engineering firms – first a company that made juice extractors for the profitable citrus-fruit trade, and later another which manufactured ventilation pipes for the coal and gold mines. He made a good living, and as we lived on the less expensive side of town, we were able to afford a three-bedroomed house with a pool in the back yard. We had good holidays, too, travelling round South Africa and what was then Rhodesia (now Zimbabwe) with a caravan and a small sailing dinghy. Like most other white South African families, we had black servants who made the beds, washed and ironed our clothes and did the dishes. We sometimes played with the servants' children – but only inside the yard. Outside our house we didn't mix. We never consciously thought much about this: like most kids, we accepted what life was like where we grew up. It wasn't until much later that I began to question the norms of South African society.

I was the noisiest child in our family. My mother used to say, "You always notice the difference if John isn't in the house." I was lively, talkative, affectionate and boisterous – and none of these qualities went down well with my father. He was a very traditional South African in a patriarchal society: conservative, phlegmatic, orderly; he was the breadwinner and head of the household, and as such he demanded respect. He got it, mainly through administering heavy-handed discipline. At meal times Andy and I had to sit one each side of him, "Just in case you need a clip round the ear".

Nowadays my relationship with my father is better than it's ever been, but back then we didn't get on. At night he would come home from work and settle down in his favourite armchair to read the newspaper, the *Star*, while waiting for my mother to put the evening meal on the table. I'd start chattering about my day at school, and he would lower one corner of the newspaper and look at me over the top of his reading glasses. One look was enough. I knew he wasn't interested in my doings, and he didn't want to be disturbed. He'd lift the paper and go back to his reading without saying a word, and I'd leave the room.

On Friday nights he liked to escape from the demands of his rowdy family and go to the pub with his mates. "Meeting the boys" was a big thing for him, and he liked to be known as a "man's man". He'd come home late, long after we had finished our evening meal, and we'd hear the car turn into the drive and stop. Then he'd get out, whistling, slam the car door, stop to water the tree in the front garden, and then fail to get his key in the front door. "Open the door!" he'd shout, and march in, demanding his dinner. Of course, it had dried up in the oven, and he'd reject it and say that he was going out to the takeaway to get a burger. Andy and I would beg to go along, but my mother would never let us – she knew he'd drunk too much to drive safely, and we'd hear the screech of his wheelspin as he set off, trying to catch the place before it closed. Quite often he'd come home empty-handed and have to beg my mother to cook him eggs and bacon.

One night he was especially late home, and my mother loaded us all into the car and drove to the pub, but she wouldn't go into the men-only public bar. I volunteered to go in and ask my father to come out, though I was terrified by the place. I made my way across the smoke-filled room guided by the sound of his raucous laugh, while all around me men in various stages of intoxication talked, laughed, fell off their bar stools or argued loudly. I delivered my message nervously and hurried out.

I knew what drink could do to people. One evening I saw a black man stagger drunkenly down the street and walk straight into a concrete lamp-post. He stepped backwards, evidently thinking it had attacked him, and went for the post like a prize-fighter, punching and kicking it. He finished off with a tremendous head-butt, knocking himself out, and fell backwards like a sack of potatoes. I could hardly believe my eyes.

I wanted to be a "man's man" like my father. As the third child in the family, I found it hard to establish a position: Carol was the first-born; Janice was the baby; Andy was the first boy; but there wasn't anything special about me. One weekend my father borrowed the flatbed truck from work and took Jimmy and Andy to the Formula 1 Grand Prix at Kyalami racetrack. He said I was too young to stay overnight with them, so I had to stay home with the girls. Yet when I took refuge with my mother, Andy used to tease me and say I was "a mother's boy". That used to whip me up into a rage, and even though I was smaller and lighter than Andy, I'd end up trying to fight him. My father said, "John, you fight like a bandit," because I never held back – I'd use fists, feet, even my head in my determination to come out on top.

It used to infuriate me that my father never seemed to chastise Andy, even when he started a fight; it made me feel as if I was always in the wrong. The only time I had my father's full attention was when I was in trouble. He could pull his leather belt out of his trousers at lightning speed, double it over and whack my rear end, which he used to say was "directly connected to the brain". Eventually I began to develop a rebellious streak. Getting into trouble was a way of getting attention, and when I was called up by my father or the school Principal for the inevitable discipline, I tried to look as if I didn't care.

In many ways I needed the discipline they tried to teach me: I had a talent for getting into mischief. They called me "Fingers Delaney" because I was always touching and breaking things. My parents used to say, "Look with your eyes, not with your fingers." I was always quick to act, and never thought about the consequences. When our pool was being constructed in the yard, some peach trees were felled to make room, cut up and piled neatly to be transported to the dump. Andy and I decided to set fire to the leaves, but the fire took hold faster than we expected, and in a few minutes we had a blazing inferno.

"Quick! Get some water!" shouted Andy, so I ran into the maids' room and grabbed a container. I didn't realise it held the fuel for their Primus stove until I threw the contents onto the flames, which leaped up with a roar. Fortunately the neighbours called the fire brigade, who put it out before things got really out of hand.

Another time Andy and I decided to make a go-kart using a soap box. The only wheels available were on Janice's new Fisher-Price doll's pram, so we cheerfully sawed them off and built a machine that was the envy of the neighbourhood. When my father found out he told us to bring our best toys to the garage. We laid out a display of our favourite dinky cars, and he presented Janice with a hammer and told her to smash the lot. "I'm strict but fair," he used to say.

Most of our mischief wasn't intentional, though. My grandmother Biddy had a large copper bowl, big enough for a child to sit in. She used to spin us round on the wooden floor of her apartment, and we had hours of fun. We wanted to copy her, as we had wooden floors, too, but we had no copper bowl, so we did our spinning on my father's antique 78-rpm LPs. We managed to scratch most of his valuable collection, and we paid the price: I couldn't sit down for several hours afterwards. Another time we let off a whole string of firecrackers very early one Saturday morning. Our big mistake was not realising that our father had a hangover from the previous night's drinking, and waking the sleeping bear on his day off, when he already had a headache, was not a good idea. We got the end of his belt again.

However, nothing curbed my sense of adventure. As children our favourite playground was the old mine workings not far from our house, part of the great gold vein known as the Witwatersrand. There were working mines a little further on, where migrant labourers worked deep underground, drilling, digging and blasting to reach the gold; some of my friends' fathers worked in the mines as supervisors. This area was deserted, however, full of disused buildings, abandoned mineshafts and great spoil heaps of yellow sand. We used to throw stones down the mineshafts and listen to the echoes as they bounced off the walls. One day as we all ran past an old shaft I hid from the others and then staged a "falling" kind of scream as if I was tumbling down somewhere very deep – they all rushed back calling my name, absolutely terrified, and I was able to jump out and surprise them. We chased each other up and down the sand mountains and hid among the outbuildings, and in the high summer, when it rained every day, we used to swim in the deep pools of rainwater that collected in the hollows – we called them slime dams.

My mother hated us playing there because it was so dangerous, but even when we said nothing she always seemed to know where we'd been. It was a long time before we realised that the tell-tale yellow sand gathered in our pockets, and collected under the garden tap where we used to wash our bare feet.

One constant thread in our family life was regular churchgoing, which provided another kind of discipline in our lives. Andy and I were the youngest altar boys, and usually our father looked us over before we set out for church in the morning, combing our hair and making sure we looked presentable. One day he had a meeting before church, so we were left to our own devices. Andy said he knew where there was some styling gel we could use, but he somehow managed to get mixed up and put toothpaste on our hair. The priest gave us some odd looks every time the two stiff-haired, peppermint-scented servers came near him.

Part of being a Roman Catholic was the ritual of Confession: the whole family went every fortnight. The priest sat in the small wooden confessional and we had to kneel on the other side of the partition and admit our sins. When the priest met my Uncle George in the street he said, "George, why haven't I seen you at confessional lately?" "Well, Father," replied George, "I don't want to seem to brag about my exploits." The challenge for us children was to tell the priest something that sounded plausible, but not so serious that he'd give you a big penance and make you recite loads of prayers. I never really thought of myself as a sinner, so usually I made up something acceptable, and he'd tell me to recite the Act of Contrition. In fact I'd never managed to learn it, so I just used to say "O God I'm sorry for my sins" and leave it at that. One day I was in the confessional just before my mother, and I accidentally farted and left a smell in the booth. That day the priest gave me a whole list of prayers to say, and my mother gave me a clip round the ear for nearly gassing her.

Church wasn't very interesting, even when you were serving. Sometimes my father read from the Bible, but mostly it was boring hymns and a lot of talking. Things seemed a lot livelier at the Afrikaans Pentecostal church down the road. You could look through the windows and see the people dance and wave their hands in the air, and there was always a lot of shouting. My mother used to say, "Those Pentecostals, shouting at the Devil!" and pull us away. We knew we shouldn't have anything to do with the Pentecostals because they were different from us; we were taught that as Roman Catholics we were the elite – the only ones who would get to heaven.

I found religion rather confusing: there were lots of rules about what you should and shouldn't do, but I never realised that you could talk directly to God and ask him for guidance (and expect an answer!). Nor did I realise that you could look at Jesus to see the kind of life that pleases God. In fact, I didn't see why we needed Jesus at all. I knew that God made the world, he made me, and he made all those rules. And if you did something wrong, and broke the rules, you prayed to Mary to mediate with God for your forgiveness. I didn't think much about where Jesus came into it.

What little I did understand I picked up at

Catechism classes on a Saturday. There I met other Roman Catholic boys of other nationalities, Lebanese and Portuguese, and we used to have running battles against the "Boers" or Afrikaners. It was my first introduction to the tribalism that affected South African society, quite apart from any issues of race between black and white. There was a distinct division between the Afrikaans-speaking whites and the English-speaking whites.

CHAPTER (2)

Schooldays

IN SOUTH AFRICA the age for starting school is six, but for some reason I started when I was five. This may have been the source of my problems at school: all I wanted to do was play at home in the garden, and I resented the time I had to spend at a desk. This never changed throughout my school life; I failed to achieve the highly regarded School Matriculation Certificate, and left with no qualifications.

My first school was the Mayfair Convent, where I was taught by the Irish Sisters of Mercy. However, after two years of falling school rolls and failing finances, the Convent stopped teaching boys, so I was moved to the local state school, Robertsham Primary for English-speaking children. This was the first time I came into contact with Afrikaans-speaking teachers. They preferred to work in the Afrikaans schools – which were always better funded and better equipped – but when all those posts were filled, they sometimes had to teach in English-speaking schools. I found it hard to understand them. Our lessons were conducted in English, but we were expected to learn some Afrikaans. At one stage my father tried to get the whole family to speak only Afrikaans on one evening a week, to help us at school. It was a good idea, but it quickly died a death because my mother couldn't speak the language at all. With only one year of schooling in South Africa, she had never picked it up. You could always get by in English.

It was a big step when I moved on to the Sir John Adamson High School: from being at the top of the primary school, I was now at the bottom of a much bigger school, and I was the youngest in the school by a year. All the more reason to have to prove myself. I wasn't helped by my appearance. I was swamped by my new school blazer (Mum always seemed to buy school clothes two sizes too big), and I had my usual home haircut (fortunately done by my sister Carol rather than my clipper-wielding father) – but my biggest problem was my bike. Dad insisted that he had always cycled to school so I must do the same, and he bought me a new bike that definitely wasn't my choice. It had a purple frame with bright yellow mudguards, a chrome carrier for my satchel, straight handlebars with white rubber grips, and no gears. The idea was that I had to prove that I could act responsibly and take care of my belongings before I would be allowed a proper racing bike like my brother and all the other kids had. I was mortified – especially as we weren't allowed to ride in the school grounds, and I had to wheel this monstrosity to the bike shed in full view of my classmates. They laughed.

After a while I hit on a solution: I was going to run to school. I could have caught the bus, but it left far too early, and I wasn't going to miss out on precious sleep time, so I hoisted my satchel onto my back and set off. Day after day I jogged down the street and out of my mother's sight before swinging off the road and taking a short cut through the mine dumps where we used to play. I knew the area like the back of my hand, so I was quite safe, but I didn't think Mum would appreciate it.

Running to school not only gave me an excuse to abandon the hated bike, it also brought an extra bonus: I got incredibly fit. I realised that athletics was something I could succeed at, and I began to enjoy sport more than anything else. I held the record as the fastest freestyle swimmer in the school, and was made captain of both the school swimming team and the cross-country team.

It was just as well I had those achievements to my name, because my attitude to my studies hadn't changed. I hated school work and only wanted to mess about with my friends. The education on offer wasn't exactly wide-ranging; in addition to the basic subjects I chose to do accountancy and art. I was hopeless at accounts, and though I was good at drawing I couldn't write essays. I scraped through the exams somehow, but in my second year (unknown to my parents) I changed from the academic to the practical course, which was less demanding. We were known as the "Spanners", because we spent a lot of time on wood-work projects and fixing things round the school. One day we spent a double period working on an old red tractor. I'd spent two weeks of my holidays ploughing on a maize farm, so I thought I knew what I was doing. I was driving it off the rugby field when I accelerated too enthusiastically, and narrowly missed flipping it over and hitting some students who were passing.

In Standard 7, I failed the Afrikaans exam, which you had to pass in order to move up to the next standard. The friends I started school with moved up without me, and I had to repeat the year. When I got my report card I prayed that my father wouldn't kill me with his belt, but fortunately he was ill that day and I escaped the beating.

I got plenty of other beatings at school, though. Some of the teachers said that I had learning difficulties, but I knew I didn't. I could grasp what was being said, but I was no good at writing things down in exams, and when I was made to go over and over the same work I got bored. I was caned so often that other kids at school used to come up to me to ask which teachers gave which punishments – they knew I'd had them all.

By this time I had a reputation as a hellraiser to keep up, and I did what I could to keep my fellow-students entertained and the teachers on their toes. Poor old Mr Cooper, the maths teacher, was partly deaf, and wore two hearing aids. I used to get all the other students in his class to co-operate by keeping totally silent, then I'd go up to him and mime as if I was talking, waving my hands and moving my lips. He'd say, "I can't hear you, Delaney," and keep turning up the volume on his hearing aids. Then I'd suddenly shout, "Watch out!" and deafen him. He'd pull out the aids in a panic, and I'd be sent off for the inevitable punishment. Once I kept him and his class confined to their classroom by spraying the windows and door with the fire hose.

I was always causing trouble, and always willing to take on a dare – often without thinking much about what I was doing. As a result I was also quite

accident-prone, frequently suffering the consequences of my own actions. One evening when we
were due to leave for a school trip, I decided to take
on the legendary school ghost, and a group of us went
ghost-hunting through the dark corridors. A sound of
footsteps in the distance made us run for our lives,
and I managed to break several windows with my
elbow, and then fall down a manhole, bruising my
legs. I had to nurse my self-inflicted injuries in
silence throughout the trip, so the teachers wouldn't
find out I was responsible for the damage. I got into
fights; I almost severed the side of my finger in wood-
work class; I cut my head doing tricks on the trampo-
line; I lacerated my arms and back in some thorn
bushes when I nearly fell out of a moving car. In one
year I had 23 stitches after my various accidents. My
father couldn't think how to curb my activities.

He decided that joining the Boy Scouts would
give me some discipline, and, although I was embarrassed to admit it, I enjoyed the hiking, camping and
boating. I had one great friend, Brett, and we spent a
lot of time together – we even cut ourselves with
knives and mixed our blood, saying that we were
"blood brothers". The Scout leaders called us "Double
Trouble" for obvious reasons. Both our fathers were
heavy drinkers, and we worked out a method of stealing alcohol from their drinks cabinets. We decided
that if our parents ever noticed the levels in the bottles going down, we would blame the maids. We used
to pour our stolen drink into plastic bags and fasten
them inside our water canteens, for extra refreshment during route marches.

Brett's mother and brothers were Christians, and tried to get us boys interested: when David Wilkerson, the American gangland preacher, came to South Africa, they took us and a group of friends to hear him speak. I was fascinated by what he said, but I knew it didn't apply to me, because he was a Protestant and I was a Roman Catholic. All my life it had been impressed on me (along with a lot of other assumptions I later abandoned) that Catholicism was the only true faith. When they tried to get me to pray with them, I refused. I was still getting dragged to Mass every Sunday by my parents, and I felt that was enough praying for anybody.

By the time I was fifteen I was going out to pubs with Andy. I was underage for drinking so I always kept a soft drink by my side as well as the alcoholic one – then if I was asked my age I could pretend I was only drinking the lemonade. Andy had a mobile disco, so he went to a lot of parties, and he let me tag along too, to see if I could pull any of the nice-looking girls. Some of these parties were pretty wild – the southern suburbs of Johannesburg were notorious for being rough areas, and the boys prided themselves on their tough and aggressive reputations. One night there were two "open house" parties in the same street, with students from two rival schools in the area. I was sitting outside with some friends and a few drinks, when a fist fight broke out in the house. The girls started screaming, and people were running out into the road, when suddenly two shots from a handgun exploded into the night. I stood up to see what was happening and saw a man running down the road brandishing a Second-World-War Luger pistol. He ran up to me and shouted, "My daughter's at that party! Who's shooting?" I pointed down the road at the other house: "It came from down there!" He ran off towards the other party, but by then people had come out from both houses, and fist fights were breaking out all down the street as the rival groups met up, fuelled with alcohol and excitement. Soon the police arrived with dogs, and we thought it was time to make a getaway – when we drove off there were so many of us in the car that I was hanging on to the outside.

When I reached 16 it was clear that I was not going to pass any exams. I'd achieved Standards 7 and 8 in the practical stream, so I changed back to the academic stream and retook Standard 8. The boys I'd started school with were now two standards ahead of me, and I never got to Standard 10, the level for Matriculation. The year before you left school you registered with the South African Defence Force (SADF), and I was keen to register, because I wanted to be a soldier. School held no interest for me, but I loved Hollywood war films, with their glamorised view of guns and fighting. I thought it was something I'd be good at. Anyway, it all seemed a long way off. For a teenager in South Africa, life was all *braaivleis* (barbecues) under sunny skies, driving round in a Chevrolet, drinking and pop music. *Saturday Night Fever* was showing in the cinema and *Staying Alive* was our theme song – we never thought we'd have to take it seriously.

CHAPTER 3

A Land Divided

MY GREAT-GRANDMOTHER Ouma was born in 1886 – the year gold was found in the Transvaal. The stories she told us as children covered the most dramatic period of South African history, from before the Boer War. She could remember visiting Paul Kruger (President of the Transvaal from 1883 to 1900) at his stately home, and sitting on his knee eating cookies and drinking ginger beer.

It was partly Paul Kruger's determination to defend the rights of the poor Boer farmers that caused some of the deep divisions in the South African society in which I grew up. Those divisions included not only the apartheid which separated white from black, but the language division between the whites who spoke Afrikaans and those who spoke English.

Afrikaans has its roots in the seventeenth-century Dutch brought to the Cape area by the Dutch East India Company. It developed into a separate language spoken by the descendants of the original Dutch, German and French settlers who became known as the Boers. They put down roots in their adopted country, and their attitude to the black races developed out of their traditions of slave-owning, and a series of "Kaffir wars" on the eastern borders – wars in which they enlisted the help of the British.

Later they came to resent the role of the British in their country (not least because the British had abolished slavery in their own territories) and many of them made the Great Trek north into the republics of Transvaal and Orange Free State, while others stayed in the two British colonies of Cape of Good Hope and Natal.

When gold was discovered in Witwatersrand in the Transvaal, and the new city of Johannesburg sprang up, the prospectors came into conflict with the Boer farmers. In 1887 the British tried to occupy the area and gain control of all this mineral wealth, but they were fought off by the Boers. Kruger's attempt to deny the vote to *uitlanders* (outlanders) and limit their influence in the Transvaal ensured that the British would not give up easily. The Boer War, fought from 1899 to 1902, devastated the country: Britain's "scorched-earth policy" burned homesteads and fields, and Lord Kitchener forced the Boer women and children into concentration camps, where thousands died from starvation and disease. Britain's eventual victory united the two republics and the two colonies under its rule, formalised in the Union of South Africa in 1910. For many years afterwards the British were seen as oppressors by the Boers: the British High Commissioner for South Africa encouraged immigrants from Britain and ruled that all education should be in English. The Afrikaans-speaking Boers saw English as *die vyand se taal* (the language of the oppressor). They struggled to retain their own language and their cultural identity as a people – the Afrikaner *volk*.

Throughout the 1920s and 1930s this Afrikaner movement grew. The National Party wanted political independence from the British Empire, economic protection for South Africa, and equality for the two languages of Afrikaans and English. When it gained power in 1948 it made both languages official, but effectively reversed the previous situation. Afrikaans became the dominant language, used for almost all the business of government, administration and bureaucracy; the police and the armed forces operated entirely in Afrikaans. From 1961, when South Africa finally broke away entirely from Great Britain, declaring itself a republic and leaving the Commonwealth, English was viewed as a lesser language (and native African languages were not considered at all). English-speaking schools like the ones I attended were underfunded; it was the Afrikaans-speaking schools that had the best exam results and the elite sportsmen, because they had the best teachers, equipment and coaches.

The National Party also enforced apartheid with a series of laws designed to ensure the total separation of the black and white races. In 1949 mixed-race marriages were prohibited; the following year the Immorality Amendment Act made all sexual relations between white and other races illegal. At the same time all South African citizens had to be classified and registered as White, Native or Coloured, and the Group Areas Act provided for forced resettlement, allowing the government to segregate people into different areas according to their ethnic background. Separate amenities had to be provided (not necessarily of the same standard) for whites and non-whites; five "ethnic" universities were set up, and non-white students were barred from all other higher education.

By the time I was growing up in Johannesburg, all these laws were in force, and so, in my world, apartheid was the norm. You might imagine that such comprehensive segregation would mean that I never saw a black person, but of course this wasn't the case. There were plenty of menial jobs that white people didn't want to do, and black people who were willing to do them. The fact that non-whites were not allowed to live in a white area was a problem that could be surmounted. Black townships grew up outside the cities, and the blacks travelled by bus or walked in to their place of work.

Most white families had live-in maids who would do the housekeeping from Monday to Friday and travel home at weekends. A separate set of enamel bowls, plates and mugs would be kept under the sink for the use of the "native girls" and "garden boys", so that the whites wouldn't catch any germs from them. Often these maids, who spent all week caring for white children, were the mothers of families themselves – they had to leave their own children at home in the care of a grandmother so that they could earn money to feed the family. In rural areas, the children were seldom able to attend school, but worked on subsistence farms or herded the cattle; they were usually illiterate. There were more schools in the townships (and a few Mission schools in the bush), but under the Bantu Education Act they all followed a restricted curriculum, effectively ensuring that black children would never have the same educational opportunities as whites.

Black families were invariably split up for most of the time. If the father was lucky enough to have work, he would often be away from home for eleven months of the year, living in a dormitory with other male workers, and doing an unskilled job for a minimum wage.

Unlike the white suburbs, most of the townships had no water, electricity or sanitation; in some townships there would be community toilets for every couple of hundred people. Some houses were built of brick or breeze blocks, but others were put together from boards and corrugated iron. Coal or wood fires were used for heating and cooking, but ventilation was poor and the homes were usually overcrowded: such conditions encouraged sickness, and lung diseases and tuberculosis were rife.

The tribal religions had their own explanations for such things. One common belief was that illness and misfortune could be brought by an evil spirit called a *toklosh*. It was small and couldn't climb, so it was a tradition in many township houses to raise the beds up on bricks or concrete-filled paint tins, to keep the sleeper out of its reach. Such beliefs were despised by many of the God-fearing whites, whose disdain included all aspects of black culture, even the well-established tribal systems with their ancient laws. For them, black culture had nothing to teach the whites, but they were not prepared to share their own educational advantages.

They also despised mixed-race South Africans, who were defined as "Coloured". In spite of the laws prohibiting marriage or sexual relations between black and white, their existence indicated liaisons disapproved of in a segregated society. My grandmother told me a joke: she said, "A teacher asked her class of children, 'Who made the Whites?' and a little girl answered, 'God made them!' Then she asked, 'Who made the Blacks?' and another child answered, 'God made them, too!' Then she asked, 'Who made the Coloureds?' and a little boy at the back of the class answered, 'The soldiers of the Queen!'" The Coloureds were excluded by whites and blacks alike – people used to call them "God's stepchildren".

In spite of the oppression and poverty which restricted their lives so severely, the Africans were generally proud people, who worked hard to retain their dignity. Even the poorest would dress as smartly as possible, and those who could afford to send their children to school would work miracles (in homes without running water) in turning them out in their school uniforms with immaculate white blouses and pressed tunics and shorts. I admired the friendliness and openness of the blacks who passed our house on their way to the bus terminus: the migrant workers were identified by their coloured wristbands. Our live-in maid had taught us some words of Fanagalo, a mixture of several African languages which enabled people from various tribes to talk together. I used to greet them, "*Sawubona, Baba*" ("I see you, Father"), and they would reply, "*Sawubona, mufanna*"("I see you, young boy").

On Sunday afternoons our white suburbs would be patrolled by the South African Police Pass Units. The white officers wore blue uniforms and were armed with handguns and *sjamboks* (whips); the Bantu officers wore brown uniforms or tracksuits, and carried batons. They were on the lookout for offenders against the pass laws, which required all black people over 16 to carry an identity document, or pass book. Domestic workers had a special pass allowing them to be in the white areas, and on their day off they used to congregate on street corners with their friends; they couldn't sit in the park because there were "Whites Only" signs on all the benches. The police were looking for their husbands or boyfriends who might have come in to visit them – they couldn't get off the street because homeowners could be fined if they allowed an "illegal" to stay on their property. The "Black Maria" police vans would cruise the street to collect up the transgressors, who faced a night in jail and a hefty fine in the magistrates' court on Monday morning.

One day I was riding my bike on the pavement when a white policeman came running up and stopped, out of breath. Clearly he'd been chasing an illegal visitor who had managed to outrun him.

"Hey, Lighty," (little boy) he said, "where's the rest of my unit?"

I pointed down the turning where I'd seen the rest of the police gathering. "The other cops are down there," I said. He grabbed my bike from me and threw it on the ground. "We're policemen," he said, "not cops."

"Cops," I repeated, and he slapped the side of my head so hard that I fell down on top of my bike. I was glad when he walked off. The police were often brutal, and anyone who got on the wrong side of them could easily get a beating. Most white people turned a blind eye to the bruises and injuries the blacks would receive in jail.

Growing up in this kind of environment, it was hard to resist the casual, unthinking prejudice that was all around us. I knew many Afrikaners who were deeply religious, led good, moral lives and upheld traditional family values – yet they had this one blind area, that they believed totally in white supremacy. In their homes, the blacks had to call their sons *klein baas* (small boss). In some ways, our family was unusual, because my parents' Christian belief and church background (and perhaps my mother's English childhood) made a real difference to their attitudes, and they tried to pass this on to us. In lots of my white friends' households, the maids' children used to play with them in the yard, but they would never be allowed in the house. My mother used to let them come in and watch television with us.

Once, she left me and Andy in the car while she picked Janice up from a friend's house. The week before, we'd seen an older boy throw eggs at some black people waiting at a bus stop, and we thought we'd copy him. We didn't have an egg, but there were plenty of stones around, so we got out of the car and collected some. When an old black man walked by on his way home from work, we threw them at him. To our surprise, he walked up the path and knocked on the door and complained about what we'd done – that in itself was extraordinary; mostly a black man would take whatever treatment was handed out to him, even by a child. My mother was furious with us. She apologised to the man, and said, "When your father gets home, he's going to give you the hiding of your life!" He did.

She also wouldn't let us refer to blacks as *kaffirs*, though that was the usual term used by white kids. I heard of one little boy who answered the front door and saw an Indian man standing there. He had never seen an Indian before, and called to his father, "*Pa, daar is 'n kaffir hier met 'n wit man se hare by die deur.*" ("Father, there's a black man with a white man's hair at the door"!)

Our church even dared to defy the apartheid regime by running a multiracial weekend prayer retreat. We all went, my father, Andy and I sharing a dormitory with black men, and my mother and the girls in the women's accommodation. We ate and worshipped together with people of different colours, something that would never normally happen, and it made us realise that people are much the same, whatever the colour of their skin. My father also supported a church society that took aid into Soweto (South Western Township). He had a monthly travel permit from the authorities, allowing him to enter the township, but as a white man he was often followed and checked by the Security Police.

I don't know how far the government saw the churches as a threat to apartheid – probably this sort of activity was pretty limited. There used to be a joke about a South African called Van der Merwe, who went to the USA for an operation. He died but was resuscitated. He was invited to Moscow, where the Russians offered him $2 million to tell the world that there was no God. He refused. Then he was summoned to the Vatican, where the Pope offered him $5 million to tell the world that he'd seen God, and God was a Catholic. He refused that, too. On the flight home to South Africa a fellow passenger asked him why he had refused all this money. Van der Merwe replied, "You wait and see how much the South African Government will give me to keep quiet, when I tell them He's black!"

I suppose our attitudes were slightly unusual for a white South African family, but I can't pretend that I was very different from the other children of my age. My friends, my schoolteachers and everyone around me accepted segregation as the norm, and I didn't have enough knowledge of the world outside South Africa to realise that things could be arranged in any other way. Radio and television (TV was introduced into South Africa in 1976) were under government control and, like the schools, were used to propagate the ruling party view, though the press and higher education were freer. All schools, whether English-speaking or Afrikaans, gave the same account of South African history since the Boer War: the imposition of apartheid was the only way for a superior minority, the whites, to run the country. It was the duty of every white South African to defend the Fatherland from any threat, whether from outside or inside.

In the 1970s and 1980s the greatest threat was seen to be Communism: the *rooi gevaar* (red danger). South West Africa (now Namibia) was effectively part of South Africa, and Angola, on its northern border, was Communist. White Portuguese refugees were flooding into South Africa with horror stories of the war there, telling how their families had been separated, women raped, and their property seized. South Africa believed it had to be ready to repel this threat from its borders. Linked to the *rooi gevaar* was the *swaart gevaar* (black danger), whether the blacks were terrorists from outside the country or troublemakers within.

The brainwashing about our duty to be in the military and defend our country started very early, at Veld School. Veld School was like a school trip – everyone went, and we spent a week listening to lectures, camping, hiking and doing sports and other outdoor activities, which I loved. The indoctrination was very subtle. They taught us a lot of history, explaining the importance of the Cape for economic survival, and describing past threats to the country's welfare (including, of course, the attempts by the British to seize control not only of the coastal areas, which enabled trade, but the mineral wealth inland).

The Boer War was at that time only 60 years in the past, and still vivid in the memories of the old. The English had called the Boers "Rock spiders" because of the way they used their knowledge of the terrain in the years of guerrilla warfare. The Boers called the English "*Rooinekke*" (Rednecks) and never forgave them for the atrocities of massacres and concentration camps. These names were still current, and we shouted them at our enemies after school to start a fist fight.

The same lessons were reinforced during the rest of the school year through the school cadet programme which prepared us for the military (all the boys spent time on the firing range, learning to use a .22 single-shot rifle). We had brown uniforms and practised drill and marching round the school field: I had a loud voice and managed to get promoted to be Drill Sergeant. Every Wednesday we had Youth Preparedness, which was a mixture of personal and health education, career advice, and, of course, emphasis on absolute loyalty to the government and our duty to do our National Service.

Andy was two years older than me, and joined up first: he did his basic training at 1st South African Infantry Battalion. He used to come home when he had a weekend pass, and on Sunday night the whole family would go and see him off at Johannesburg railway station. I couldn't wait for it to be my turn to go; I was bored at school, and the only things I knew I was good at were sports, physical fitness and fighting. They ought to stand me in good stead as a soldier, I thought. The platform would be full of young men in uniform, all returning to their divisions, and sometimes I recognised the maroon berets and wing badges of the South African airborne troops, known as the ParaBats because they were in the Parachute Battalion. They were my ideal: known as an elite unit who took only the best candidates, they stood tall and proud. I wanted to be part of a unit that had a reputation like that, for pride and resilience, for unity and cohesion, for fearless fighting. I promised myself that when the time came for me to do my duty for South Africa, I'd fight for my country in the best battalion there was.

Conscription

WITH WAR BREWING in Angola, the government had increased the duration of National Service for all white South African males from one to two years. In addition there was a National Reserve period: for ten years afterwards, you could be called up for camps lasting up to three months each year. By the mid-1980s, the South African Defence Force could deploy 400,000 white operational personnel in the space of two weeks, including Permanent Force members (the professional armed forces), two-year National Service men and the Citizen Force commando units available for camps. It was a highly trained, effective fighting force, and by the time I was 17 I was impatient to join it.

When the registered letter brought my initial call-up instructions, it told me to report to 7 SAI (South African Infantry) in July 1980. I wrote back requesting to join the January intake at 1 SAI, as I wanted to be close to 1 Para Battalion. No one was ever called up directly to the Bats; you had to volunteer from your allocated unit during basic training. So in January 1980 I joined hundreds of school-leavers at Johannesburg railway station. The whole family and my girlfriend came to see me off; I'd been anxious because we were late setting off for the station, but my father just said, "Don't worry, they won't leave without you!"

He was right. That first day I was to find out the army motto, "Hurry up and wait". I said my hurried goodbyes and was ushered into line with all the other new recruits, where we waited while the Military Police (commonly known as Meat Pies) searched our bags for drugs, weapons or alcohol. At last we were marched off, only to wait again while we were each given a styrofoam container covered in clingfilm. This was our introduction to army food: a massive slice of bread, a dried-out sausage, a hard-boiled egg, a tomato and an apple. It was all washed down with a cup of tea. When at last we were loaded onto the troop train, we crowded to the open windows and beat the coach sides like drums – we were off!

We were all excited and no one wanted to sleep, though it was an overnight train journey. As we passed through small-town stations some people threw pillows and blankets out of the windows to the tramps and beggars on the platforms – they seemed grateful, though our gifts often knocked them over as they landed. We arrived in the early morning at Bloemfontein, where we were loaded into open trucks and taken on a jolting journey over rough roads. Five kilometres away from the base, two of the trucks broke down, and we had to push them the rest of the way, with our army instructors shouting abuse at us. I couldn't believe they were the same nice, helpful guys who had shepherded us onto the train the day before.

From the moment we entered the base all the orders were given in Afrikaans; most of the Permanent Force members were Afrikaans-speaking.

The Sergeant Major said, "The first 50 years in South Africa were English; now the next 50 years will be Afrikaans." My Afrikaans had always been poor, but now it got better fast – you were expected to respond to an order immediately, and you couldn't do that if you were still translating it in your head.

Three thousand troops from all walks of life were assembled at the huge infantry base. First we had the dreaded haircut, a great equaliser. One guy had long hair and a beard, and they did half his trim and sent him back to the end of the line (accompanied by shouts and whistles from the rest of us) to queue up again and get the rest of it done. Then we were issued with our kit: a steel trunk with sheets, blankets and a pillow, to stand by our beds in the sleeping tents. Uniforms, boots and bush hats (supposedly fitted for size, but sometimes on the basis that "one size fits all"). Rifles and cleaning kits. "Your rifle takes the place of every relationship – mother, father or girl-friend," said the instructor. "And it's a rifle, not a gun." Rifle in one hand, we shouted after the instructor, "This is my rifle; this is for shooting," and with our private parts in the other hand we shouted, "This is my gun and this is for fun!"

We knew life in the army would be hard work, and it was. Endless marching on the parade ground, which was holy ground to the drill sergeant, and tough on those troops who had two left feet. No privacy: there were communal showers, which had to be cleaned thoroughly every day, and no doors on the toilets (toilet paper was so precious it was known as white gold). Queuing up for meals, eating off stainless-

steel dishes called "pig pans". Jumping when someone gave you an order, and learning that instant obedience was the only response. Lessons in Afrikaans,
trying to understand and take notes and not fall
asleep because it was a rare chance to sit down.
Cleaning and kit inspection, cleaning and tent
inspection, cleaning and toilet inspection, and a fist
fight afterwards because someone hadn't done it
properly and the whole tent had failed; physical
training and marching, marching and more marching.

All you had for company was the rest of your platoon of 30 men – most of them under 20 and away
from home for the first time. No wonder the mail call
was so important. You had to do push-ups in
exchange for every letter you received – and love let-
ters (with perfume or lipstick kisses on the envelope)
were extra. It was great when parents sent parcels
with treats – biscuits, sweets and *biltong* (dried beef
sticks). Even if you didn't get on that well with your
family, suddenly you realised how much you missed
them. One Saturday afternoon we were listening to
Forces Favourites on the radio, and someone had asked
for the sentimental record *Soldier Boy*. There wasn't a
dry eye in the house.

Gradually we were being transformed from laid-
back teenagers into a fit, disciplined fighting force.
We left behind our individuality as we were moulded
into soldiers; we were trained to submit to authority
and obey orders instantly; we were proud of our
country, proud of our army, and proud of our role in
it.

1 Parachute Battalion

One day about two months into our basic training, we were told that anyone who wanted to volunteer for a specialised unit had to report to the hall. Commandant Moore was asking for volunteers for the ParaBats. "I can only promise you hard training and loads of action," he said. All the Parachute Battalions came under the command of 44 Parachute Brigade; 1 Parachute Battalion had eight full-time rifle companies. Two were fighting in South West Africa: one deployed as a "Fire Force" reaction task group at Ondangwa Air Force Base, and the other involved in vehicle and foot patrols, known as Sweeping Operations, in Sector One-Zero, the Operational Area. At the end of the 1970s 1 Parachute Battalion had played an important role in the bush war in Rhodesia (now Zimbabwe). This was just what I wanted: the more action, the better. I signed up for the selection tests the next day.

Officers and NCOs from the battalion tested us for fitness, co-ordination, strength and speed, and I got through – fortunately I'd managed to get Standard 8, the lowest education level they would accept. I rang my mother in great excitement: "I've been selected for the Bats!" Then I packed my kit and cleared out of 1 SAI. It was a fantastic feeling as we drove in through the gates of one of the finest fighting units in the world.

This time I was joining 600 other volunteers from army, navy, air force and medical services; we were placed in "Delta" and "Hotel" companies. From the first moment we had to run everywhere – only senior officers had the privilege of walking. In the first week one young recruit suffered a minor heart attack from the exertion. Our hair was cut even shorter – a "number four" – so we all looked like prisoners.

We ate in the mess tent, and on the first day I sat opposite a self-confident *troep* (soldier) who was sharing out the bowl of food between the six of us at the table. He caught my eye and said, "Hey, what are you looking at, man?" It was the kind of thing that could easily start a massive punch-up, and I could see this big guy knew his business. Still, I was never one to back down, and when he saw I was prepared to stare him out he swung a huge hand towards me and said, "Howzit, my name's Gungie." We ended up good friends.

Once again we were allocated platoons and issued with kit: for the first few months we wore brown overalls each day, and we had green infantry berets to wear with the smart "step-out" tunics that we wore to church parades. Then we started training, running round and round the parachute-packing house, over and over again until we moved like one man. We learned to carry a man and his weapons and kit, because the ParaBats never left a man behind. Each day finished with an eight-kilometre run, and on Fridays we ran through the obstacle course, too, swinging on the Tarzan ropes, and crawling through tunnels and over cargo nets and under barbed wire. We got fitter and stronger, though some recruits couldn't stand the pace and were RTU (Returned to Unit) even before the final tests began, bitterly disappointed at having failed.

All the physical training was designed to equip us for the final gruelling two-week PT course. On the first Monday we were kicked out of bed at 04.30 hours, and dressed in thick airborne battle smocks which we would wear all day in the hot African sun. The instructors took bets among themselves about how many recruits would drop out at this stage. The long sessions included running, leopard crawl, chin-ups, the obstacle course, carrying men and weapons, long-distance runs (42 kilometres), route marches, and rolling across sand after drinking lots of water. We were given 30-kilogramme concrete blocks called "marbles", which we had to carry with us while training; you would often see tears of determination trickling down the face of some young recruit as he emerged from a tunnel full of mud, pushing the hated marble ahead of him.

The instructors drove us on, but not as hard as our own determination to succeed: we were tough and unforgiving among ourselves. One day eight of us were given a 200-kilogramme airborne pallet and told to carry it on a 21-kilometre run. One *troep* kept saying, "I can't make it, it's too heavy, it's too heavy." I shouted to the *troep* behind him, "Motivate him!" and he did – we heard the slap and the thud as his head connected with the metal.

On the final Saturday we had the crucial tests which decided whether we could advance to the three-week jump course. One after another, without a break for rest, we had to carry a man and his kit in a fireman's lift, 175 metres in 75 seconds; sprint between two ropes six metres apart, 40 times in 90 seconds; and run with helmet, webbing and rifle, 3.2 kilometres in 18 minutes. For the power tests we had to do 67 sit-ups in two minutes, mount a two-metre concrete wall with full webbing, and climb a five-metre rope to touch a steel girder.

I passed, along with 80 others out of the 300 of us who started in Delta Company.

Starting the jump course had a familiar feel – but with different kit (glass-fibre Para helmets, big jump boots and a folding-stock Para FN rifle), different unit (Falcon 3, consisting of two "sticks" of twelve men each) and a different routine. For three weeks we trained in every aspect of static-line parachute deployment, rehearsing day after day until the drill was automatic. We came down slides and the 30-metre tower we called the ape cage, and we practised landing and rolling and recovering our parachute. The day before our first jump we were taken up for flight experience and stood in the doorway looking out, so we knew what it would be like, but we didn't have to jump. It was our last chance to step down from the course, if we couldn't face stepping out of that plane.

The following day we jumped for the first time from the ParaDaks. As well as the dispatchers in the plane, we had a ground instructor shouting commands through a megaphone, but one *troep* hadn't expected this, and froze. On the ground they asked him, "Why didn't you comply with the order?" He answered, "I was so scared I thought it was the voice of God!"

We had to do eight qualifying jumps. On one of

these we were jumping with personal weapons containers (PWC) strapped to our legs, including the dreaded concrete block. The drill was that you checked around and below, and then jettisoned the kit, which remained attached to your harness, dangling harmlessly beneath you on a three-metre line, so that it landed a moment before you did. In the confusion in the plane, I hadn't noticed that the pin which held it had come loose, and my marble plummeted from 800 feet into the ground below. Thank goodness no one was below me at the time. When I landed I had to dislodge it from the crater it had dug into the ground. Fortunately the Jumpmaster didn't see what happened, or I'd have been ordered to run the 20 kilometres back to base.

Another of the qualifying jumps was at night: the plane lights were dimmed and we stepped out of the noisy plane into the silent moonlight of the African bush veldt. We couldn't see anything of the drop zone, but as we descended we could feel the heat radiating up from the ground. This told us that we were only metres from impact, so all we could do was to brace in the landing position and hope for the best. Another clue was the groans we could hear, from the *troeps* who had landed moments before!

Jumping was everything I'd hoped. It was terrifying and exciting, the biggest adrenalin rush you could hope to get. There was satisfaction in knowing what to do, how to adjust your direction to make sure you were coming down into the wind (if you came down with the wind behind you, you'd hit the ground too fast: we called it a GT because it was a high-performance landing). The moment when you stepped out of the plane into nothingness, staring straight ahead (never look down!) was amazing; so was the last moment of ground rush, from about 50 feet, when the earth suddenly seemed to hurtle towards you and your whole body was braced for action. I loved it.

All our families and girlfriends were invited to our wing parade (commonly known as "glamour day"). We did a Delta Company formation jump from a Hercules C130, then we were presented with the parachute emblem to wear on our uniform, and the coveted maroon beret. We were proud of our achievement, proud of our unit and proud of our Code of Honour. Our motto was *Ex alto vincimus*: Victory from Above.

Code Of Honour of 44 Parachute Brigade
I am a proud and fully-fledged member of 44 Parachute Brigade.

I am a Paratrooper, which is second to none in the world.

I promise to wear the insignia of the Brigade with pride and distinction, and to conduct myself at all times as is required of a Paratrooper.

During battle I am first and foremost a Paratrooper and promise to behave as such, even if the enemy outnumbers us by far.

I pledge the highest sacrifice to my country should it be expected of me.

I believe in myself, my formation, and my country and, above all, I believe in God.

Off duty

After our wing parade we were given a long weekend pass, which we were determined to enjoy to the full. We had worked hard and trained hard, and although all this physical activity was demanding, once we were free from the constraints of camp we didn't have the slightest intention of getting some rest. We wanted to have some fun, preferably including alcohol, girls, and probably a fight or two. One weekend Gungie and I were driving home in a car belonging to someone else in Delta Company. We stopped at the first store we came to for beer and rum and coke, then Gungie took off his tunic and sat on the roof of the car, while I was driving without a licence at twice the speed limit. When we clipped another car we stopped and pulled the driver out of his vehicle: we looked so threatening that he said it was no bother and he could easily fix the damage. No one messed about with the Bats.

We'd all been brought up with the idea of respect: respect was what your father demanded, and respect was what you wanted for yourself. Charlie Company was the intake six months ahead of us, and they thought we should show them the same respect that we had to show Alpha and Golf Companies, definitely our seniors because they were a year ahead of us. We disagreed, and there was a massive free-for-all in one of the bungalows on the base. It was all part of sorting out status, like the order in a pride of lions.

Similarly, because we believed the ParaBats to be the elite fighting force, we only really respected our own members, who had their airborne wings. We were supposed to salute all superior officers, but once we were at a railway station where another unit was based, and their Captain came towards us on the platform. We raised our arms but didn't actually salute – we didn't want to show him respect. One night I was involved in a brawl outside a nightclub and the bouncer came out to separate us. "What's going on here?" he asked. My opponent replied, "It's the Bats; they're making trouble." The next minute the bouncer floored him with an almighty punch. "That'll teach him to mess with us Airborne," he said.

When we got back from a weekend pass the instructors chased all the "civvy" attitudes out of us by making us do physical training for the whole day. The standing order in 1 Parachute Battalion was that no troops were allowed to drink alcohol – once some seniors had been well over the limit and tried to beat up the Commanding Officer. Nevertheless, we usually managed to smuggle some drink into the base, and we'd sit round swapping tall stories of what we'd been up to. There was lots of macho one-upmanship, but it was surprising how often the stories involved guys saying they'd gone home and beaten up their fathers. Most of them had been heavily disciplined by their fathers while they were growing up, and had probably vowed that one day they'd be big enough to get their own back. I don't know how much of it was true. Certainly I'd had the same impulse, and when I went home, trained by the army to a peak of fitness and strength, I knew I could take him out whenever I wanted to. I just chose not to.

Gungie's contribution to the festivities was usually a little stash of cannabis. One night the MPs came in on a bungalow raid, and as usual we stood to attention, heads up, fists clenched at our sides, just as we did for inspection, while they searched the place. They emptied his cupboard and turned his bed over and even poked into the hollow places in the frame, but they didn't find anything. They went out and we got the order to stand at ease. It was only then that Gungie winked at me and unfolded his fist. "Hey Johnny," he said, "my stash was in my hand all the time."

When we didn't have a weekend pass we would jump the wall and go AWOL (absent without leave). We'd gatecrash the dances at the Afrikaans University and dance with the girls, but we always sent a surveillance team in first to check for officers or MPs. If the coast wasn't clear, we'd move on to the rough pub at the railway station, because no officers dared go there. We'd arm-wrestle the drunken locals for beers (we always won) and plan fights against the civilians. I felt right at home as a Bat: drinking, fighting and pulling the girls was just how I'd been spending my spare time before I left school – only now I could drink more and fight better, and I didn't have any trouble attracting the girls, either.

CHAPTER ⑤

Soldiers in Training

WE THOUGHT WE'D MADE IT when we got our wings and our maroon berets. We didn't realise that our training had only just begun, as the Bats began the long haul of turning us into fighters. The first phase covered weapons, opposing military forces, First Aid and bush craft. Every morning after inspection we would do formation drill and march for hours until we were familiar with every command. We didn't understand then how important it was that we could respond automatically to orders, and keep going even through the exhaustion, fear and desperation that is the reality in the theatre of war. When we weren't on the parade ground we were in the classroom or on the firing range or doing orientation in the bush. Every moment was occupied from morning to night. At times the instructors would come back drunk after a night on the town and wake us up and make us drill up and down the bungalow. Unthinking obedience was important: we even had a pee parade, when they made us urinate simultaneously on the word of command.

Shooting was specially important, but most of us found it relatively easy. South Africans were brought up with guns, and anyway we'd all started out in the military cadets at school. I won a badge for being a good shot, but everyone had to reach a high standard: it was essential if you meant to stay alive in the Ops

Area, where it was either kill or be killed, it was the enemy or you. We started with the folding-stock Para R1 rifle – 7.62-millimetre, 20-round magazines. Later we were issued with the lighter R4: these were 5.56-millimetre, 35-round magazines, Israeli Galil rifles. We would run from the 1,000-metre mark and fire at 900 metres and fire again at every 100-metre mark until we advanced on the target.

The second phase of training included conventional warfare, when we spent time in the bush, dug in for weeks in trenches, gaining ground and moving our foxholes forward, and then retreating and redigging. We also did urban warfare and specialist training: drivers learned how to drive the various all-terrain bush vehicles, medics were trained at the military hospital, and signalmen went off to become familiar with radio communications. Specialist weapons groups worked with mortars, machine-guns and anti-tank weapons. I was selected as a Section Leader, and spent six weeks on a course with other troops from Hotel Company.

Reconnaissance Commandos

By this time I wasn't content with being a Section Leader in the Bats; I'd set my sights on something else. When I told my mother I'd been selected for the Airborne Reconnaissance Commandos she said, "I'm not happy with you joining the Recces – the Bats were bad enough." If the Bats were known as the elite fighting force, the Recces (along with the Koevoet Special Police) were known as the most violent. I was about to find out how they got that way.

My friend Gungie had also passed the selection, so we set off together on a slow three-day train trip to Durban. After a week of training and equipping we were on the move once more, this time to St Lucia on Natal's north coast. We were first assessed by military psychologists, then assigned a number which was printed on our armband – and from then on we were known only by our numbers. It was the ultimate technique for eradicating any individual identity and making us into what the army wanted us to be: mere cogs in a fighting machine, soldiers who would obey unthinkingly because their ultimate responsibility was to the fighting unit.

The main activity on this course was survival training. We were body-stripped and searched for food, money or anything else that might give us an advantage. Then we were divided up into sections and sent off. We had to march for many kilometres along thick sandy beaches, with two men at a time carrying old wooden railway sleepers. We were hungry and thirsty, but I had managed to hide some money in my webbing belt, so I was able to buy us some bread and cold drinks from the locals. We knew the instructors would be keeping an eye on us, so we took great care not to be followed. We used every trick in the book for "avoidance and surveillance", even walking barefoot and backwards to hide our tracks! It was no use – the instructors had been playing this game longer than we had, and they caught us and found out what we'd done. We were punished and made to carry extra ammunition cases through the swamps.

After this we flew by Hercules C130 transport to the Caprivi Strip, a semi-operational area in South West Africa. There we were made to do the survival walk again; we were given five rounds for our rifles and carried mortar-bomb cases filled with concrete for extra weight. Every five days we were given small portions of food and water, and the map references for the next checkpoint where we could get supplies. At one stage a pack of young lions tracked us until they lost interest and moved off into the bush. We'd been told to sleep with our heads facing inwards, because a large hyena could crush the head of a man in its jaws; we slept with our rifles along our bodies and pointing outwards. One night we were woken by a yell from one of our group, and saw a male hyena retreating from his lost meal. That night we built a fire like a towering inferno and slept with one eye open.

A few nights later another Bat was cleaning his rifle when a young lion made its way silently through the thicket and took a flying leap at its prey. The lion's claws tore into his forearm, but his "foxhole buddy" was able to fire off two shots, which scared the intruder away. The next day our ammunition was confiscated by an instructor, who said he couldn't have us harming the wildlife.

The next stage of our training was to be "captured" by an ex-SWAPO (South West African People's Organisation) cadre. We were marched off and made to sing enemy songs and do physical training, even though we hadn't eaten for days. Days turned into weeks and no one knew when the course would finish. We got weaker and weaker and thinner and thinner. It was in situations like this that you relied on *vasbyt* (stand fast) – the ability to grit your teeth and endure the hunger and the exhaustion and just survive. You also relied on your mates; you pulled them through when the going got tough, because you knew they'd pull you through another time. Isolated and desperate, you were being trained for what could really happen in war.

Gungie and I were doing all right – we could have made it as Recces – but in the end we decided not to complete the course. I was still under 21 and needed my parents to sign their consent for another three years' commitment if I was to become a Reconnaissance Commando. I knew my mother wasn't happy about it, but that wasn't the real problem. I'd seen some of the officers and instructors on the course, and many of them were wrecks. Their bodies were scarred with bullet and shrapnel wounds they'd sustained in battle; some of them had been with the unit for the maximum fifteen years. Most of them were hard drinkers, and very few of them had wives or families. They seemed to lead strange, one-dimensional lives, in which their involvement with the training wing was their only interest. I wanted to fight, but I didn't want to end up like them. For the first time I could see that the romantic image of the professional soldier had its downside; this didn't measure up to the Hollywood glamour I'd dreamed of.

It was strange, because in many ways I was ready for another challenge, physically, mentally, and emotionally. Yet I wasn't sure I wanted to sign up for more years of training and fighting, when I hadn't even completed my first year of training. I said to Gungie, "We're still young; we've got good lives and girlfriends to go back to. Maybe we'll come back when we're older and give it another shot." Amazingly, he agreed with me, and we both stepped down. Our Senior Officer was disappointed with our decision, but he placed us in a temporary bush camp before sending us back down to Durban.

We had one more evening at the Recce camp before we went back to 1 Para Battalion, so Gungie and I went out on the town. We visited several drinking holes, and Gungie bought some cannabis and slipped off for a joint. He was walking back towards me when I saw a car following him slowly along the street. We got talking with the occupants, who said they were just out for a night on the town. One of them asked how we were going to get back to base, since it was after midnight.

"That's no problem," said Gungie. "I'll smoke this joint and then I'll easily be able to run the eight kilometres back." Suddenly they all jumped out of the car brandishing nine-millimetre handguns: they were undercover narcotics-bureau officers. We'd been out in the bush for so long we'd forgotten our old streetwise habit of keeping an eye out for the police. One of them was just telling me not to move or he'd shoot me, when Gungie threw a punch at one of the others and took off down the road, scattering the hash behind him. They eventually caught and handcuffed him and put him in the back of the van.

Then they picked up all the cannabis from the road by the light of their torches.

Gungie was charged at the police station and sentenced to be caned. It was a serious punishment: the police would put a leather gag in your mouth, and cover your legs and back to protect them, then cane your bare backside. When we went back on the train the next day, Gungie couldn't sit down.

Coin Ops

While we were away on the Recce selection we had missed some of the urban warfare training, but we got back for the counter-insurgency operations training, known as Coin Ops. It was designed specifically to deal with the threat to our borders from surrounding countries. After the defeat of Germany in the First World War, South Africa had been nominated as the governing power to take over the former German South West Africa. Now the people of South West Africa wanted to be freed from South African rule, and their resistance fighters, known as SWAPO (South West African People's Organisation), were being helped by infiltrators entering Owamboland from southern Angola. Our mission was to terminate their advance and cut off their logistics support. The freedom fighters were trained by the Russians and Cubans in Communist Angola, and they were determined and well equipped.

Together with another sharp *troep* I was allocated the job of scout. We were issued with an American M79 40-millimetre grenade launcher, which was ironic, since South Africa was subject to an arms embargo by the United States. Once again we started the endless repetitive training which would ensure that, when we were involved in the real thing, our responses would be sharp and automatic. We did "jungle runs", with simulated firefights using live ammunition: our instructors would shout orders from the rear as targets appeared ahead of us and we practised our quick-kill technique. We advanced in "fire and movement" formation, odd and even numbers moving forward alternately. Once we had secured the killing zone we took cover, reloaded our weapons, checked for wounded and then went back into the contact area once more and did "overkill", putting two bullets in each dead man's head. This was a security precaution: sometimes the enemy would pretend to be dead, but unpin a hand grenade and place it under their body. When someone came and turned the body over, the spring would be released and the grenade would explode, killing both *troeps*.

We learned a snap firing technique which involved keeping both eyes open and sighting down the side of the barrel (faster than lining up the sights) while discharging the weapon. You hit your target with a double tap, two bullets to the head to make sure it was a kill. There was no room for error: it was kill or be killed, the enemy's life or your own. We had no doubts about how close we were now to the reality of war, and the question in every *troep's* mind was, "How will I react under live fire in the Ops Area?"

We were already getting closer to the action, but my first real experience wasn't against the rebels in South West Africa, but against the blacks in my own country. We were sent to guard the Pelenoni Government Hospital, because there was trouble in a nearby black township. Riot police had been brought in to control the uprising with tear gas, rubber bullets and occasional live rounds, and the casualties were being brought into the hospital. A crowd of blacks gathered outside, wanting to know what had happened to their injured families and friends, and we had to force them back and keep the way clear for the ambulances that were still arriving. As a government hospital for blacks, it was understaffed and under pressure, so some of our medics were helping the staff as they stitched and bandaged the wounded, and others helped in surgery; some of the victims died on the operating table, and two of us were on duty carrying the bodies to the mortuary. We were only supposed to deal with those who died in the hospital, but one ambulance driver wanted me to sign for someone who had died on the journey, to save him going all the way to the city mortuary.

I had to put swabs of wet cotton wool on the eyelids of the corpses to keep their eyes closed. Apart from a road accident I'd witnessed as a child, I'd never seen a dead body before – now there were dozens all around me, and I was glad to have the company of the black nurses working there with me. Then, suddenly, one of the bodies behind us gave out a huge moan; we spun round just in time to see it collapsing back onto the table as if it had been sitting up. One nurse screamed and ran across the room, and my heart was racing. The other nurse laughed and told us it often happened. There were other sights which made an impression on me – a man who had bled to death after a road accident in which he was crushed between two cars; the people outside the hospital who wanted to mourn their dead, but who were being kept out by the soldiers; the dilapidated state of the wards where the wounded lay – but I didn't let it affect me. I was a soldier, and I had a job to do. In the military our highest aspiration was to do our duty and serve our country, and we were glad of the opportunity to do that. We got over such experiences by making a joke of them.

It was harder to joke about the deaths of our comrades. Charlie Company, the intake six months ahead of us, had completed their training and were now on active service in Angola. One unit had reported enemy movement near their position, and were told to attack without further surveillance or air support. They had underestimated the size of the enemy force, and lost two of their men in the ensuing battle. Delta Company slow-marched at their funeral. In the old South African National Anthem we pledged our service to our country,

In ons wil en werk en wandel
Van ons wieg tot aan ons graf

In our will, our work, our striving
From the cradle to the grave.

It was certainly true of the young soldiers who believed totally in their loyalty to their country, and who could be pushed hard in battle because they thought they were invincible. It wouldn't be the last grave we would stand beside, looking proud and impassive, as the trumpeter played the Last Post and someone's mother wept.

In December, Delta and Hotel companies were deployed in an airborne "show of strength" parachute drop into the Caprivi Strip in South West Africa. I'd already been there for my survival walk with the Recces. We were dispatched with full personal ammunition, eight litres of water, food rations for five days, sleeping kit, and ammunition for our "stick" (ten men) – grenades, mortar bombs, anti-tank rockets, machine-gun rounds and my grenade launcher. We had to do a 500-foot "hop and pop" bush jump (so called because of the low altitude: you hopped out of the plane and the canopy popped open immediately). Some troops were injured in the landing: I narrowly missed a tree stump and a pool filled with the summer rain. One officer was shouting instructions from above, and we looked up to see him caught by his parachute in a thorn tree – when the chutes were dislodged he fell and broke his collarbone. My friend Dougie landed on the seat of his pants and compacted his vertebrae. The used parachutes were collected and the injured were evacuated, then we had a route march, following map co-ordinates to our designated location, dug in and set up radio communication with HQ, who sent us out on patrols.

It was during this time that I reported sick with severe chest pains. I'd been feeling tired for a couple of days, but suddenly I had no energy at all and I could hardly breathe. I was taken to Mpacha Military Hospital and given a bed next to a soldier from 32 Buffalo Battalion, a black unit. Only white South Africans were conscripted for National Service; blacks were not expected to fight for the country in which they were not allowed to vote. However, some volunteered to enlist, and they had their own black battalions. Normally all hospitals were segregated, but as he was a soldier he was of course brought into the Military Hospital. His wounds were infected and I could smell the gangrene in his leg, but the doctors seemed to be ignoring him. I had just been admitted with all my kit, and I still had my rifle with me. I turned it on the medic and said, "Come and treat this man or I'll use this weapon. Whatever your views on race, he's still a South African soldier." They took the man away – and while I was asleep, they took my rifle away, too. When I woke up they told me the soldier had been treated.

I was diagnosed with inflammation from a heart infection – quite a relief as I thought I was having a heart attack. I was given an injection in the fatty layer around the heart, and returned to my unit.

We had now completed the final stage of our one-year training. We went home at Christmas for a week's leave, and some well-earned love and attention from our families and girlfriends. My brother, Andy, two years ahead of me, had completed his basics in National Service and enlisted as a professional soldier in the Air Force. Trained as a flight mechanic on the Mirage F1 fighter jet, he had been accepted as a Flight Engineer on the Alouette helicopter gunship, where he finished top of his class and gained the rank of sergeant. He had already been involved in active service when the jets were deployed against installations in Angola; now he was going back into the Ops Area to wreak havoc with 20-millimetre cannon. When I went back to join my unit, I, too, would be a fully operational soldier fighting for my country. My mother now had both her sons trained to kill in the South African theatre of war.

CHAPTER ⑥

Sector One-Zero

THE PREVIOUS DELTA COMPANY had gained a reputation as a mean fighting company, and we were determined to live up to it. In Falcon 3 we had two sticks of twelve men; my stick included my mates Gungie, Dougie, the Fox, Kojak, the Green Machine, and Stan the Man. We were a close-knit group who had trained and worked together and we all looked out for each other; in the months of action that followed we proved ourselves again and again, relying on each other in battle conditions and becoming the best fighting unit in the company.

In January 1981 we flew from Bloemfontein to northern South West Africa (SWA), to be deployed in the Ops Area on the SWA–Angolan border known as Sector One-Zero. The main town in the area was Oshakati, which had hospitals, schools and colleges; Ondangwa Airport, to the south-east, dealt with both military and civilian flights. Up here on the high, dry Huila Plateau the land was covered with dense thorn scrub with hardly any trees. The terrain was semi-desert and the soil was thick sand, in which vehicles were always getting bogged down. As we disembarked from the large transport aircraft with all our kit, we realised it was several degrees hotter up here than it had been in South Africa. The glare from the white sand was dazzling, and we reached for our sunglasses.

There was no doubt that we were now close to a war zone: Bravo Company had just returned from a mission where they made contact with a group of SWAPO insurgents. They had eight kills, which were being placed in body bags ready to be transported to Oshakati and identified. It was the first time I had seen so many dead with camouflage uniforms and weapons of Russian origin, and it made me wonder what it would be like to be fighting against this determined, Communist-funded army. Bravo Company looked unconcerned; they were sitting among the dead eating energy bars.

We were given accommodation within the perimeter of the Ondangwa Air Force Base, close to the helipad. We had four-man tents, with underground bunkers for safety when under attack. The first night we were there we heard the 40-millimetre anti-aircraft guns open up: eight guerrillas had approached the perimeter fence, and the guns were providing ground cover fire for the group of Recces who counter-attacked and killed them.

We were installed as a rapid-reaction force known as "Fire Force", which consisted of four Falcon groups. Each group had two sticks of twelve-man assault teams, deployed in a Puma helicopter. Our standing orders were to wait for infantry patrols to make contact with the enemy in the bush; they would report back and then we would be airlifted into the killing zone. We were fresh, well-armed and able to move fast; we could take over from the foot soldiers who had invariably been in the bush for up to three weeks. Not only were we super-fit; we were keen to encounter the enemy and ready to kill.

Fighting units measured their performance by their "kill rate", and we wanted to be the best. A soldier couldn't afford to think about the enemy as a person, as an individual with a family and a life worth living. A soldier could only see the enemy as a threat and a target: a threat because he would kill you if you didn't kill him first, and a target to be killed and added to the impersonal score. That was our training, and if it dehumanised the young men who were conscripted into the army, that was how it was designed to work. That was how you achieved success in war.

Every day we had morning parade and a situation briefing before we completed our routine chores. Then it was a case of waiting until the siren sounded, when we grabbed our kit and weapons and ran to the Puma helicopters. We would be briefed in the air, en route to the "kill zone".

Our first mission was search and rescue: a pilot had ejected from his Impala jet after a sortie in Angola had gone wrong. The Air Force were especially concerned because this was one of their own, and we were scrambled in two Puma choppers. The helicopters lifted off, rotor blades cracking the air, and we gained height swiftly over the runway and bore away towards the map references we had been given. We waited tensely inside: it was our first venture into this volatile border area, and we didn't know what awaited us, or whether there would be fighting. We had machine-gun teams covering both doors, and two Alouette helicopter gunships following us, ready to hover overhead and provide top cover with their 20-millimetre cannon and bird's-eye view.

The navigator took us straight to the spot, the pilot eased us in low and the flight engineer turned, gave us the thumbs-up and shouted, "Go!" We jumped out into a whirlwind of dust kicked up by the blades, and deployed immediately into the all-round defence formation, scanning the bush for any enemy movement. The helicopters moved off at once: after the drop the unarmed Pumas were vulnerable targets. We found the pilot and the medics stabilised him. Both his legs were broken, so they called back the Pumas for casualty evacuation ("cas evac"), and we accompanied him back to base to wait for our next call. Dougie and Kojak stayed behind to guard the wrecked plane overnight until vehicles could come and recover it.

Some afternoons we were deployed into *kraals* (local farm homes), rounding up suspicious-looking young men who didn't have the appropriate identification documents. We would take them back to Military Intelligence to be interrogated, as that was the way we got a lot of our information about the movements of the enemy forces and how much support they had in the area. When walking patrols we had different formations depending on the terrain. In dense bush we would walk closely in an extended line within eyesight of each other. One day we were advancing on a *kraal* when we heard a shot; one *troep* was convinced that a sniper had taken a shot at him and hit the ground just where he was about to put his foot down. We reported back and the gunships gave us cover, blasting the bush to shreds – we didn't fire at all – but there was no response. Later on someone thought to check the soldier's rifle: it smelled of cordite. We realised he had accidentally pulled the trigger and discharged a round himself, almost shooting himself in the foot.

Our next mission was to search and destroy a group of guerrilla infiltrators; we had received reliable information that they planned a mortar-bomb attack on Sector One-Zero headquarters in Oshakati, using 122-millimetre red-eye rockets. Delta Company was deployed in vehicles with orders to check out all possibilities, but without harming the civilian population. Days went by and no attack materialised, and we were getting bored, so we decided to make things happen a little faster. Protected by the mortar and machine-gun teams we entered *kraals* and did routine searches and interrogations. The means were often brutal but always highly effective, and we managed to gather information on the whereabouts of the intruders. In one search we found a prosperous young man with a collection of banned liberation propaganda leaflets. We held him over a large drum and beat him; he told us about an arms cache in the north of One-Zero area. The Koevoet Special Police investigated and found a stockpile of weapons.

We took advantage of the innocence of the youngest children by bribing them with sweets to talk to our interpreter. They often gave us valuable information about enemy movements and the arms caches they had in the bush, without realising what they were doing. Sometimes as we entered a village we would see small boy running away, going to warn the occupants of the next village that we were coming

– the bush telegraph in action. Once a teenage boy ran away from our patrol, and two of us chased him, sprinting with difficulty in the thick sand. When we caught him he wouldn't talk, so we held him over the side of the vehicle and took him for a joy ride through the bush until he was willing to speak. It was a cat-and-mouse game with the enemy; during the day we would question the locals about infiltrators, and at night the guerrillas would come out of the bush and get information from the same people about us. The civilians were always caught in the middle between our opposing forces. As far as I was concerned the enemy was fair game, but I did feel some regret about our treatment of the innocent people trying to live peacefully while surrounded by guerrillas and soldiers waging war on each other.

By March we were given orders to search and destroy the SWAPO "Typhoon" commandos who came into the Tsumeb area every year to infiltrate the white-owned farms. We were working with the Koevoet Special Police, who had their own fierce reputation to keep up (their name means "crowbar"). They would only work with the "Bats" because our reputation approached theirs; they trusted us to run the spoor (tracks) and fight and shoot well. In one contact a police warrant officer (who had joined this crack team from the Recces) ordered us to stand up and shoot our rifles on automatic. It was an effective fear tactic and caused a large group of the enemy to break cover and run. He later had a 50-calibre Browning machine gun mounted on his Caspir troop carrier; he had a cassette player and used to play the

Queen song "Another One Bites the Dust" at top volume when advancing into battle. There was a rumour that the Koevoet got paid for every kill in the bush – certainly when we brought the body bags into the forward control bases after every contact, they bought us beers. We used to enjoy our evenings together in the protection and comfort of the military base.

Delta Pipeline

The Delta Pipeline was a passage of dense bush which provided cover for the infiltrators along the line of a vital water-supply pipe, and our job was to seek out and destroy any enemy groups in the area. On 1 April we had picked up tracks, and by midday our anti-landmine vehicles were in hot pursuit. We made radio contact with One-Zero and we were quickly gaining on a 90-strong enemy force that was "bomb shelling" – splitting and regrouping continuously to avoid contact. When they realised they were outrun, they knew they could only turn and fight, so they laid an ambush. As we were approaching them we met up with the SADF motorcycle platoon that had been following another section of the enemy that was regrouping into this larger force. They stood down then: the Bats and the Recces always had priority, and could go anywhere within the One-Zero area.

The rest of our group was travelling in three armoured vehicles, being guided on foot by a bushman tracker, and I was part of a three-man ground team protecting him. As we approached the enemy ambush, a rocket was fired. It struck the armoured windscreen of one vehicle, was deflected upwards and airburst 270 metres above us. My training kicked in and I realised that I was exposed, out in the open in a real live contact – the situation the seniors had spoken about and for which we had trained for months. Instantly the commands ran through my head, as clearly as if someone was shouting them at me: dash, down, crawl, observe, sight and fire. We hit the ground in the middle of a maize field, and I twisted to lie sideways along the furrows. The young maize plants were only about 30cm high and didn't provide much cover, but it was the best on offer. I could hear the battle raging ahead and behind me as volleys of mortars and various other weapons rattled and roared.

The vehicles sped off in pursuit of the fleeing enemy, but we three runners and the tracker were left stranded on the ground with our ammunition supply depleted. The tracker had a big 7.62 weapon; we carried 5.56-calibre rifles, as their lightweight magazines enabled us to carry twice as many rounds, but they were almost shot out. The other strength of our weapons was that the rounds had a tumbling action, which caused severe damage in the body of the target – if they lived, they usually developed gangrene. As we cautiously made our way forward into the bush I kept checking the ground areas, front, middle and rear, looking from right to left (that way the eye picks up more) with my ears pricked for every sound. The tracker signalled that there was a SWAPO commando hidden directly ahead, then shouted, "SWAPO, shoot, shoot!" as a shot whistled past me. The tracker couldn't shoot: I was ahead of him and blocking his line of fire. I spotted the sniper's position, really close to me, and reacted instantly, firing the double-tap, two rounds from my rifle, sighting down the side of the barrel for speed, and aiming at his head. I saw the rounds make contact, but to my amazement the guy stood up and started moving away. I realised that the small-calibre round hadn't been effective: at such close range it was travelling so fast that it hadn't had time to perform its damaging tumbling movement. I let go with another burst from my weapon and then kicked out at the man with my foot. Just then the tracker arrived and finished him off. We moved on to the next infiltrator and silenced him, too, and then regrouped with my stick.

We had a routine on the battlefield: after you had been through a contact area, you first checked on your comrades, then reloaded your weapon, then went back to do the overkill – two shots to the head on each body to make sure it was dead. Then you checked the bodies for papers, money or valuables, and took some personal memento. I took some Angolan money from my body, and later put it in an album I kept. If anyone looted a body that was your kill, you would fight them: you took a possessive pride in what you'd done. On this day we tied the dead bodies of the enemy on the back of the vehicle and returned for an overnight stay at a forward base in the Ops Area; we had not lost a single man.

I was the first man in Falk 3 to get a kill, and it made me a hero. It was what we had trained for, and it gave me a thrill, a feeling of exhilaration and power. At the same time, I knew that behind this there was a kind of weakness. You could train as a soldier, you could act big and talk big like everyone else, but the question at the back of your mind was always whether, in a real situation, you would be able to kill. At last that question was answered for me: this was a real war situation, this was a real soldier, and I'd killed him. Now I was a grown-up, and I had the admiration of my mates. It was a good feeling. I'd killed my first man – and I was 18 years old.

Sporadic battles went on for days as we made our way through the dense bush of Owamboland, beating the enemy out with sheer persistence backed up by superior weaponry, vehicles and logistics. Yet survival could also be a matter of luck: one day we were sent off without the Koevoet to check Charlie Pipeline. Back at Delta Pipeline three Koevoet police officers triggered a trip bomb placed on the path by insurgents entering Tsumeb. All three were killed.

In the evenings we went back to Inanaha Base; we lay on the wall with our weapons facing out, ready for an enemy attack, and watched the beautiful African sunset. One night when we were off duty after supper, they showed a Hollywood film. It wasn't very good, and I lost interest and was thinking back over the day's events when there was a shoot-out on screen. Without stopping to think I dived off the bench and took cover – then looked around to see that everyone else had done the same! Our reactions were instant, automatic and identical. We laughed, but I wondered whether I'd ever be able to relax and do something as ordinary as watch a film again.

CHAPTER 7

War in Angola

ONE OF OUR REGULAR ACTIVITIES was running airborne raids on SWAPO bases in Angola. The Air Force
would go in first and bomb the area, and we would
follow in our helicopters. As we sat inside the Puma I
would look round at the camouflaged faces of my
mates and see the same look of serious tension everywhere. No one would admit to being anxious, but the
same thought was in every mind. Would this be just
another day in Angola, or would this day be our last?
When travelling in the Puma the machine-gun team
sat by the open doors with their weapons facing outwards, and the rest of us sat inside with our weapons
pointed downwards. This was so that any accidental
discharge couldn't damage the rotor blades and cause
a crash; you were always aware of how vulnerable you
were in a helicopter.

In Ops Ceiling my Falcon group was involved in a
pre-dawn attack on a *kraal* where we knew some top-
ranking enemy officers were meeting. We moved in
under cover of darkness, led by an informer, and took
up position outside the perimeter fence, with our
rifle barrels pointing in through the posts. As the
first glimmers of light showed in the sky, a rooster
crowed and the camp began to stir. No order was
given, but we all began to fire simultaneously, scattering the officers. Those who were not injured by the

high-velocity rounds tried to run away, but we pursued and brought them down. That day we gathered valuable logistical information, orders and maps for the area, which we passed on to Military Intelligence for use in future hunt-and-destroy missions. Eight enemy officers were killed. Usually we removed the bodies of the enemy, carrying them on our vehicles out of the contact area, but if the journey was long we sometimes buried them in shallow graves (you don't want dead bodies on the back of a truck for long in the hot African sun). We couldn't airlift them out as there wasn't room in the helicopters.

We occasionally had to make a tactical withdrawal. One day we were informed by an old man that there were SWAPO fighters in the area who had been bothering his daughters. We requested gunships from HQ and set off on foot, but we soon picked up spoor of chevron-patterned boot prints, and decided to follow these, though the man was beckoning us in a different direction. We soon came up to a small, fast-moving group of enemy soldiers, and terminated them all with the help of our gunships, though the man was shouting, "Not SWAPO! MPLA!" When we regrouped with the rest of our company, we heard that we had attacked an Angolan Military Reconnaissance Group; we were ordered to return to the border, 30 kilometres away, as fast as possible.

Enemy BTR 152 armoured troop carriers were in the area on a seek and destroy mission, and they would attack any SADF troops in the area ten kilometres north of the "cut line" of the border. We were running low on ammunition and knew we couldn't withstand a mechanised attack. Sure enough, soon one of our observation posts reported that the BTRs were coming; we were told to run south, attempt to regroup after four kilometres and head for the border. Even as we fled, we encountered several small SWAPO groups and had skirmishes with them from which we emerged intact. Eventually, just as we reached the border, our Air Force jets scattered the pursuing vehicles.

After weeks on patrol we were glad to get back to Ombalantu Base, but life there wasn't particularly peaceful. There were plenty of fights because of inter-unit rivalry or personal arguments; one sergeant was attacked with a screwdriver because he had killed another man's pet kitten. Our anger was always ready to erupt and everything had to be dealt with by physical violence. The army had turned us into fighting machines, and we couldn't be switched off easily. We noticed the difference later when we were on patrol with an infantry platoon from the Citizen Force – men who had done their National Service like us some years earlier, and had been called up for one of their short annual tours of duty. We were supposed to set this group onto some spoor we had been tracking, but when I pointed to a boot imprint the officer stepped on it and said to his troops, "Can any of you see spoor?" When I tried to argue with him he said, "Look, most of us are married men, with families and jobs. We don't want to play war games." I realised that those men had lost their fighting edge. We were always aware of the urgent threat of the Communist insurgence and our duty to protect our country, but those older conscripts had regained a civilian mindset.

Operation Protea

We went off for three weeks' training in SWA to prepare for our next encounter, and anxiety levels were particularly high – we had been told to expect a well-equipped enemy and high casualties. We had to act as though we weren't afraid: we used to sing, "If I die in the combat zone, box me up and send me home", but we couldn't avoid thinking about death. People react in different ways to threats like these. Most *troeps* were pretty hard drinkers; several used cannabis when they could get it, and I saw one man mainlining heroin which he had stolen from the medical supplies in a raid. They say that there are no atheists in the trenches, and I met several people who put their faith in God. In our battalion we had a group of Pathfinders, whose job was to be deployed first into enemy areas and mark out the drop zones for the rest of us. To do this they were trained in "hi-lo" freefall – the plane came in high for safety, and they made a high-altitude exit, but a low-altitude canopy opening to avoid detection. It was a dangerous activity. One of these guys told me that he had been a drug addict, but finding Jesus had changed his life. He told me about his faith, and helped me to pray a salvation prayer, asking Jesus to come into my life. I went along with it, but it didn't mean much to me. I did pray secretly: I told God that if he got me out of that operation alive, I would serve him – though I don't think I really knew what that might mean. It certainly

John, aged four. Note the blond hair.

John at 16, with Scruffy.

Delta Company PT course on the cargo nets, with battle smocks, helmets and water bottles.

Company jump with rifles from Hercules C130.

"Black is beautiful" for night manoeuvres. Note the RPG7.

John, Gungie and Dougie airborne by helicopter for a base raid in Angola.

Arms caches burning at the start of Operation Protea.

The captured town of Ondjiva. The enemy base was a five-kilometre series of trenches and bunkers surrounding the town.

We gained valuable intelligence from this captured officer.

Walking out alive: John and Gungie, safe after weeks of fighting in Operation Protea, August 1981.

Baptism in a Rhema swimming pool.

Our wedding day:
Tara and I were
married on 6th April
1991.

Graduation night, 1991: the end of two years' Bible school, three hours every evening after work.

Street march: John carries a cross through the streets of Hillbrow and Johannesburg.

Crossing a bridge, previously blown up in the war, on my way to a crusade in Angola. It was an amazing feeling to be going back with a message of peace.

A street march in Angola.

On the road to Mbuji-Mayi, Zaire (now the Democratic Republic of Congo).

Crusade in Mbuji-Mayi. I had never seen such an awesome crowd. We estimated it to number more than 300,000.

On the road back from Mbuji-Mayi!

didn't change the way I behaved, and I didn't want to be seen praying or reading the Bible. In the army, it's really important not to do anything that marks you out as being different from your mates.

We were about to go into some of the fiercest battles we would see. Operation Protea was aimed at two strong MPLA bases in southern Angola, Xangongo and Ondjiva, and waiting for us were tanks, anti-tank guns and five kilometres of concrete bunkers. The Communist Angolan government had obtained support from sympathetic nations around the world: there were 23,000 Cuban troops deployed in the country, with Russian and East German officers training and equipping the MPLA. These would not be border skirmishes against pockets of guerrillas. This was war against a well-equipped army.

We crossed over the cut line at night and drove until dawn. The enemy radar had already been destroyed, so our aircraft had free movement; our Canberra and Buccaneer jets dropped 500-kilogramme bombs on the targets, and the Mirage F1s continued the assault with a volley of rockets. We came into battle formation in our open-top vehicles, defended by 90-mm guns on the Ratel troop-carriers. The Storm Pioneers joined us with their 122-millimetre mortars pumping shells into the distance, and the artillery were firing their 140mm recoil guns. Then we were given the order to dismount from the vehicles and proceed on foot, flanked by two infantry battalions. There was artillery ahead of us, with their anti-aircraft guns firing at our planes, so we tried to take them out. I saw acts of great bravery on the battlefield: one Falk 4 *troep* on the advance line took a direct hit, and as he fell the man beside him dived onto his wounded friend to cover him, shouting for the medics. I realised that our training in teamwork and our fast responses were keeping us alive.

Overnight we withdrew to regroup under cover of darkness, but the next day we were harassed by snipers. We had to take cover wherever we could, and at one point three of us sprinted for the same tiny hole in the ground. We all squashed in together, laughing, then silenced our assailant. Our biggest problem was a large Cuban anti-aircraft gun that was dug in – it had 23-millimetre machine-gun barrels and was destroying everything in sight. We were pinned down for over six hours. Every time we terminated one gun crew, another would climb up and continue blasting away. We were in radio contact, and eventually we were told to withdraw 50 metres for safety – only an air strike was going to take out this troublesome gun.

The call sign from ground communication to the Mirage F1 is "Miracle", and that was what it seemed like as two supersonic jets came in for a strike. The ground shook as the bombs exploded and we all wondered if 50 metres was really enough distance to withdraw. The following two aircraft fired rockets, but then we heard one pilot warn his buddy that he had a surface-to-air missile on his tail. We stared into the sky as the pilot headed towards the sun at incredible speed and released his explosive missile deflectors, then banked in a 110-degree turn as the missile carried on and detonated.

We were still pinned down by the artillery, but our commanding officer was tired of inaction. He ordered our machine guns to fire on the target and commanded Delta Company to charge. With only our rifles for cover we charged forward, firing on the target as we went, and managed to overrun the gun emplacement at last. After that we were told only to fire if we could sight the enemy, but I could see a single enemy soldier running away from me at about 500 metres. I placed my sights on the distance position and opened fire. I saw him lift off the ground as the round made contact, ripping his uniform off his body. One more down to me.

Over the following days we continued to advance, clearing out the trenches as we went. You couldn't let a single enemy soldier remain hidden – a support *troep* sleeping in his foxhole had his throat slit by an enemy commando who slipped in during the night. One vehicle-recovery technician knelt on an anti-personnel landmine and had his knee and part of his face blown off. Three of us blew up an arms cache that was stored in a massive bunker known for booby-traps. We tossed in our grenades, turned and ran: we had 4.5 seconds to get clear, but as we fled through the bush it felt as if we were running in slow motion – I was sure we would never get far enough. The shock of the first detonation gave me an added boost, and I suddenly developed a turn of speed like an Olympic sprinter. The subsequent firework display went on for hours.

One day we found a large, dark, underground accommodation bunker, so we tossed in two percussion grenades and went in. Inside we found eight stiff enemy troops lying on their bunks, who we supposed had died of their wounds from the previous day's fighting. We gathered clothes and weapons into a heap on the floor, detonated some white phosphorus grenades to start them burning, and ran for safety. Once outside we heard coughing coming from the bunker, but a quick headcount established that we hadn't left anyone inside. Then the "dead" bodies came stumbling out of the bunker, choking on the poisonous gas: they had pretended to be dead in the hope that we would ignore them and go on our way. We could have shot them then, but we saw that one had officer insignia on his lapels, so we handed them over to Military Intelligence.

We were pulled back for a while to Oshakati, then redeployed into the same area for ground-clearing sweep-up operations. It was more of the same: flushing out the snipers hidden among dense vegetation, walking slowly in our single line, keeping an eye open for each other. One day I was edging forward among bushes and small trees. I lifted a low branch with my left hand, with my rifle ready to fire in my right. As I peered under the branch, I saw an enemy soldier lying on his back, with his weapon pointed at me and ready to fire. I took a step back and raised my rifle, but the range was too short and there was no room to aim. I fired, and at the same moment my friend double-tapped him from the side. Once he was wounded we finished him off with more shots to the lungs and heart. It's hard to describe the exhilaration of walking into an enemy who has a loaded weapon pointing at you – and being the one who walks away.

These events were repeated endlessly over a huge area, with different battle groups operating along the lines. At the end of the nine-day battle we had captured equipment worth $200 million; over 1,000 of the enemy were dead. The only member of Delta Company who lost his life died in a swimming-pool accident back at Ondangwa base, and that affected us more than any of the death and destruction we had encountered. All the other dead bodies we had seen were black; seeing a white soldier dead, one of our own company, and not even on the battlefield, gave us a strange feeling of unease. Suddenly we all felt much more vulnerable.

Bush leave
The night before our leave was due the Entertainment Corps put on a concert, and we danced on the stage with some lovely white girls. It was a novelty, because for weeks on end we had seen only black people. We all knew the old saying, "Absence makes the heart grow fonder", but we used to change it and say, "Absence makes the blacks grow blonder".

The Chief of Staff made a speech in which he commended Delta Company for our exemplary fighting skills, which had distinguished us among all the battle groups. Of course, that infuriated the Artillery Reserve, whose tents were alongside ours, and there was a lot of heckling and abuse that night, and pencil flares were shot at our tents. Miraculously, we restrained our natural impulse to go over and sort them out; we didn't intend to jeopardise our precious and well-earned leave.

We flew back to Bloemfontein in September to a heroes' welcome and a parade through the streets alongside other fighting units. Then we checked in our equipment and got a lift home in a pick-up truck. After the heat of Angola the cool South African climate was a shock, and the closer we got to Johannesburg the colder it got; it seemed unusual even for late winter. Then, amazingly, it started snowing. I'd never seen snow before, and it made the whole journey seem even more bizarre. We met up with some mates from Delta Company and had a snowball fight with some brave civvies outside the shopping centre.

My parents came back from a business trip in Europe to find me settled at home enjoying my leave. They had been astonished while they were away to see the Angolan war reported on television, as there was a press embargo at home, so details were never reported to the general public. They had been very concerned about my safety. It was strange to be back with my family – like living two separate lives. Showered and wearing civilian clothes, sleeping in a comfortable bed and eating ordinary food, it was hard to believe that I was the same person who had been enduring battlefield conditions only a few days before. Still, it was good to talk to my mother and my sisters, and they were glad to have me safely at home in one piece.

The last weeks of war

Our last leave was cut short and we were ordered back early to active duty, to take part in Operation Daisy, so once again we had to make the mental and physical transition to military life. Delta Company was back as the rapid-reaction Fire Force, sent to wait at a forward control base known as Helicopter Administrative Area (HAA). Once again we experienced the old mixture of emotions: you felt tension, aggression, horror and exhilaration each time you killed, and knew that you had escaped with your life once again. Every mission brought with it the secret fear that this might be the time you wouldn't come back.

One day it really was a close thing. We were deployed "hot" into the battle zone, so as soon as we exited the Puma and ran into the all-round defence position we came under automatic gunfire. The dust thrown up by the departing choppers was thick with the smell of cordite. One of our K-car gunships was shot down, killing a crew member, and we began fighting for ground with *troeps* of 32 Buffalo Battalion (the paid volunteers of the black battalion) beside us. The battle was getting out of control, partly because 32 Battalion was equipped with enemy camouflage and AK 47s, and the gunship pilots couldn't differentiate between them and the opposing forces. We were called to "hot extract" from the area, and detonated a green smoke grenade to signal to the incoming Pumas to airlift us out.

As our chopper landed, we bundled into it, along with some Buffalo Battalion troops who had broken rank. When we looked around, we saw there were 20 *troeps* as well as the three crew in the Puma: it was designed to take a maximum of thirteen. The Flight Engineer ordered the Buffalo Battalion out but they wouldn't budge. The Puma was struggling to lift off; it rose, then bottomed out as everyone shouted and clapped the "one, two – one, two, three – one, two, three, four, airborne!" we always shouted when lifting off the runway in the ParaDaks. The pilot pulled up again and we cheered as we took off, the belly of the aircraft scraping the tops of the trees.

In battle situations like that one you relied on your mates to stand beside you, and you knew everyone's strong and weak points. You also had to work together with other units, whether white or black, even though in civilian life you wouldn't usually meet. When we were searching for the enemy we cut the spoor with bushmen trackers from 31 Battalion, another paid black South African force. They were incredibly skilled, able to track a lion from a vehicle moving at 60 kilometres an hour. They could make a fire without lighter or matches, just by using the friction between two different pieces of wood. They were reliable trackers, but as soon as we located our objective they would run off, leaving us to fight through the contact zone without further information.

One tracker also worked as our interpreter, and we used him in a covert operation, masquerading as a single enemy operator who had been separated from his infiltrating group. We dressed him in an enemy overall and armed him with a hidden small-calibre side arm. We gave him a beating so his story, that he had been chased by our vehicle patrol, looked convincing. He managed to obtain valuable information from the locals, which enabled us to track a group of insurgents to a *kraal* and capture them.

These tracking patrols were always tense affairs; they might be quieter than a full battle contact with jets and armoured vehicles, but they were still dangerous, and you never knew where the danger might come from. Once one of my mates was shot in the arm, severing the main artery in his biceps. By the time we had managed to stop the bleeding there was blood everywhere, over our uniforms and all the kit inside our vehicle. The medics had trouble setting up an intravenous drip, as all his veins had contracted due to his state of shock. By the time the helicopter came to cas evac him, we were all stressed out. There was an old woman sitting at the side of the road by a pile of decaying watermelons, watching all this going on. As the helicopter lifted off, taking him to safety, she started laughing nervously. For some reason this infuriated me, and I jumped out of the vehicle, grabbed a watermelon, and pushed it over her head. Then I twisted the soft fruit round on her shoulders and walked off.

That kind of anger was always close to the surface, and I never knew when it would explode into action. Sometimes we spent days chasing infiltrators, our progress hampered by the guerrilla groups who would fire on us and then disappear into the bush, leaving us painstakingly following their tracks. One day as we entered a *kraal* where we thought our quarry might have hidden, we met an old woman with a broom, who was busily sweeping away all their tracks. We were furious that we were going to lose the trail and all our efforts would be for nothing. Our officer pulled out his commando dagger and held it at her throat, while the interpreter shouted, "Where is the enemy?" She closed her lips and refused to speak, and I lost control. "You won't get anything out of her," I said, and hit her across the face. Then I jabbed my elbow into her throat and kicked her as she fell to the ground. She turned her face away and a stream of blood came out of her mouth, and one of my mates shouted, "You're going to kill her!" and pulled me away.

It's hard to explain how such things could happen, except that being on patrol was like being in another world, where different rules applied, and you got used to seeing violence all the time. Plus, of course, we were driven all the time by the one imperative that had been dinned into us from childhood: our country was under threat and our job was to protect it. On one occasion we fought a furious 20-minute battle with a large group of insurgents armed with everything from rifles to a rocket launcher, and took out around 40 of them. While we were regrouping, two unarmed boys who had been hiding in the undergrowth made a dash for their lives, and a Falk 4 *troep* stood up and shot them both in the head. It was as if, once we started killing, it was hard to stop. Later we saw a young mother lying wounded beside her baby, and a *troep* finished her off with a shot. He claimed it was a "mercy killing", but he counted it as one of his kills.

This level of brutality explains some other violent behaviour: the frequency of rape. I saw this at first hand: one night four of us were dropped off for a surveillance operation, but found no detectable enemy activity. We were bored with waiting around, and crept into a *kraal*, where one of the others suggested that we rape some of the women. Fortunately nothing happened: he did grab a girl, but she took one look at him and screamed with horror, and all the dogs started barking, so we left. Afterwards we laughed about it. We had blacked up our faces with camouflage paint, but the girl must have seen his blue eyes and realised he was white. Not many soldiers were tolerant of this sort of behaviour, though. We had one interpreter – we called him "the Talk" – who we knew had raped three girls. One day he stopped a big black guy for questioning, and hit him when he wouldn't tell us anything. The guy retaliated, and the Talk expected us to defend him, but we just left him to get a beating. It was our way of punishing him for his activities.

There was no doubt that we all became desensitised among all the bloodshed – it was the only way to cope with so much death. The longer we were deployed, the more common this became. Some troops later required hospital treatment for their mental state: in the First World War it was called "shell-shocked"; the Americans in Vietnam called it the "thousand-yard stare"; we called it being *bos befok* – a state of being dazed and unfocused, a sign that the mind has switched off to protect itself from the trauma of thinking about what is going on around it.

This was the kind of life I'd been living as my date for demobilisation approached. I was still only 19 years old. I had served four terms of three months in the Ops Area, a much longer term of active engagement than was usual. For our bravery and endurance in the service of our country, everyone in Delta Company was awarded the Pro Patria Medal. Were we proud of it? We renamed it the Pronutro medal, after our favourite breakfast cereal.

Always a Soldier

AT THE END OF OUR TIME of service we said goodbye to our lives in 1 Para Battalion. We had to hand back all our equipment, so we replaced anything we'd lost by stealing items from our juniors in the next intake (they would do the same when their turn came). We were told that for the next ten years we would be required to serve at camps lasting from one to three months every year, the period to be decided by 3 Para Battalion, to which we were now allocated. Then we left.

Our military life was cut off as abruptly as it had begun; there was no counselling, no period of adjustment, no programme of rehabilitation into civilian life. One day we were fighting for our country and our lives; two days later we were back home, looking for a job. That was simply a routine transition for all the young white South African men of my generation.

At the age of 19 I was physically fit, expert in a range of armaments and a skilled parachutist, but I didn't have a single marketable skill, not even Standard 9 education. My father's advice was to get an apprenticeship – that way I would always have a trade to fall back on – so I got a job with a plumber, and enrolled at Johannesburg Technical College. In February 1982 I started my plumbing apprenticeship, with the promise of eight months' release over two years for military service. I attended two three-month courses to gain my National Technical Certificates 1 and 2, and another three-month Practical Plumbing Course at BIFSA (Building Industries Federation of South Africa). Another milestone passed in my adult life. I had a job and a degree of independence.

The independence was something of a surprise; it was the first time my life had not been structured by others – either school or the army – and I could choose for myself what to do with my evenings and weekends. What I mostly chose to do was drink.

With a group of friends I used to go for wild camping weekends at the historic mining town called Pilgrim's Rest, where gold was first discovered in the 1860s. We used to have drinking competitions that started on the journey, and we usually stayed drunk the whole weekend. We had a rule that no one should touch any alcohol before tea in the morning, so we used to boil up the water, pour the tea into mugs, and then throw it over our shoulders and open a beer.

We enjoyed our reputation as hooligans: we rode off-road motorbikes through the town, doing wheelies past the traffic officers. Sometimes we drove up into the mountains behind the town and went potholing, exploring abandoned mines, crawling through holes and slipping down mud slides. We emerged drunk, dishevelled and covered in mud, and alarmed the people at the nearby caravan park by jumping into the swimming pool all together, fully clothed. The camp site officials asked us to leave, because so many people complained about our behaviour. We were happy to go, and took ourselves off to camp in the bush. The important thing was that we were never thrown out of anywhere: being asked to leave showed us respect, and that was what we required. It was part of who we were.

In between outings I went to work, pleased to be earning my own money at last. My personality still came out in the way I approached my job: I seldom thought far ahead. One day I was working on a first-floor landing on a private plumbing job, and I called to my friend, "Let me have the hammer, will you?" Then I realised that he was working in the hall below, so I leaned over the rail to see where he was, only to be hit in the eye as the hammer sailed up to me. I fell backwards, knocked unconscious, and had to be taken to hospital for stitches. On another building site a water pipe burst, and I jumped over a wall to escape the fountain. I found myself dangling by one hand from the top of the wall, until the brick I was holding on to came loose and let me fall two floors onto a stack of equipment. I suffered my usual bruises and scars.

My basic physical fitness was always a bonus, helping me to emerge relatively unscathed from these adventures. I worked for a while on the Avionics building in Johannesburg, where a team of labourers were cleaning out a pit in the basement. One elderly worker didn't come up for his tea break, and was left down there with the petrol pump running. When we came back, we could see him slumped in the bottom of the pit, overcome by the carbon monoxide in the exhaust fumes. There was an iron ladder down into the pit, and I volunteered to go down and rescue him. I got him in a fireman's lift – he was surprisingly heavy for such an old man – and started to climb back out. Halfway up I began to lose my grip on the muddy rungs, and to feel the effects of the poisonous gas myself. Just then one of the site managers joined the group of workers watching from the top, and he shouted to me to hang on. "Are you a Bat or a mouse?" he asked, and I knew I had to prove myself for the sake of the battalion. I managed to hold on, though I wanted to bite the rungs with my teeth! They lowered a rope, which I tied round my burden, and they hauled him up out of the pit. From that day on, the black workers showed me exceptional respect: the old man I had saved was one of their Zulu tribal chiefs.

In many ways I was still very like the youngster of my schooldays: daredevil, accident-prone, and living for kicks. Now, however, there were new dimensions to my activities – in particular, the drinking made me even less responsible than usual, and the move from bicycle to motor vehicles was an added danger. My father had tried to help me by buying me first a motorcycle and then a small car, but I didn't maintain them or repair the damage from my frequent minor crashes. One Christmas holiday I stayed drunk for two weeks, and only sobered up after an accident when I was driving with three friends in my car. I approached a stop sign at high speed, the brakes failed and we shot straight across a busy street, narrowly missing the evening rush-hour traffic. We crashed into a church fence and came to a halt.

Alcohol usually makes young men more aggressive, but my anger was always close to the surface anyway. At my 21st birthday party I had a fight with my brother outside in the street; Andy was drunk, and when I pulled a knife on him he defended himself with a dustbin lid. My father and a friend had to separate us. I threatened my ex-girlfriend's new partner with a knife, too. I had broken up with her because she was putting pressure on me to get married, which I didn't want, but I didn't like to see her with another guy. My jealousy was inflamed when I'd had a few drinks, and I chased the pair of them through a shopping precinct.

I even had fights at work, sometimes over quite petty matters. I fought with a workman installing air conditioning, over some plumber's paint I'd left on his ducting. My foreman was a white Rhodesian, and he was egging me on to beat my black opponent. I managed to knock him to the floor, but he jumped up and struck me with a steel electrical conduit pipe. Zulu stick-fighting is a serious martial art, and he got in two rapid blows to my head and another on the leg, bringing me to the ground, and I knew I had to roll away fast or he would kill me. I pushed his ladder onto him and punched him, but he got out and hit me on the head with half a brick before running off.

One day Andy and I went to the redundant mines area to play Combat Paintball. The two teams took it all quite seriously, wearing combat dress and camouflage, and we joked about getting back into our old uniforms. We had hand-held weapons powered by CO_2 cartridges, with plastic-coated paintball ammunition. We had all done our military service, so we used our bush tactics for surveillance and stalking, and it was great fun. Then I managed to score a hit on one of the opposing team, but he didn't want to be "dead" and refused to leave the game. I was furious. I shot him at point-blank range on the top of the head, and said, "Now you're definitely dead." He punched me and I hit him back, and before long we were rolling around on the yellow sand, while I pummelled him continuously. I was amazed at the anger that was unleashed as I attacked him, and I realised that I couldn't really control it. After that, I decided that I was never going to play paintball again – it was too close to my Ops experience, and I knew that once I was back in that mindset I could easily kill someone. The aggression was always with me, just below the surface, and ready to flare up at the slightest provocation. Fuelled by alcohol and my need for excitement, I was ready to turn any confrontation into a battle.

The fact was that life in civvy street was dull compared with the constant danger, physical demands and excitement of life in the Paras. I had been trained for fitness and endurance in difficult conditions; now I had a routine job and a safe city life. I had been taught how to focus my aggression and become a killing machine – in my two years of action I had killed many times – handling all the fear and exhilaration that comes of facing an armed enemy; now I was expected to walk peacefully around the streets and not respond to arguments with violence. No wonder ordinary life seemed boring. All the time I was looking for something that would give me the same highs as army life – drinking, fighting, going with girls – but nothing matched up.

There was another aspect of my new life that was hard to handle: the constant nightmares and flash-backs to the war. Incidents I had shrugged off or laughed off with my mates now came back to haunt me in vivid dreams. When you watch a war film, how-ever horrific or realistic it may be, it still reflects Hollywood's romantic view of life: everything can be made to look glamorous. Battles may be noisy and bloody, but your attention is drawn to the things the director wants you to think about, the comradeship or the courage – not the waste of life. Even while we were living in the reality of war, we were caught up in the ideology of duty and patriotism which drove us on. It's only after the event, when the battles are over, that you discover that your mind has the ability to play scenes over and over like a videotape inside your head, and you can't escape from it. Traumatic sce-narios are embedded in your subconscious, and affect your behaviour.

Night after night I would wake up sweating from dreams in which we parachuted down into an enemy ambush, or I walked alone through a deserted battle-field to find one enemy still alive and pointing his weapon at me. During the day I could keep busy enough, or drunk enough, to keep the images of death away, but at night I was defenceless, always afraid that the enemy could creep up on me. I took to sleeping on the floor under my bed, where I felt safer. In the mornings my father would come and call me for work, and I would roll out from under the bed and spring up, instantly alert, holding him off with one hand, with my hunting knife raised in the other.

"What's the situation?" I'd say.

"Situation normal," he would reply. "Now get up and go to work!"

After a moment I would register where I was, wake up properly, and put the knife down.

My mental state was made worse by feelings of guilt. If I closed my eyes I could still see the old woman I hit with my elbow and knee. When she vomited blood I knew she would die, but I did nothing about it. All I thought about at the time was my frustration at getting no information out of her. Now her lined old face haunted me. Another kill of mine was a 16-year-old boy. He was an enemy soldier – often quite small children were abducted in Angola by their own people, indoctrinated and made to march with the army and carry a gun. I felt guilty about what we had done to some of the civilians who crossed our path, but mostly I managed to retain my soldier's attitude that shooting soldiers was OK, just part of staying alive in a war. Still, when I saw kids of his age in the street I remembered how young he'd been, how small his lifeless body had looked. He'd had no more choice about fighting in that war than I had.

That was why I filled my life with partying, drinking and fighting, seeking temporary escape from my suppressed anger, vivid memories and relentless guilt. Yet at the same time I could see that I was on a downhill path, living a life that had no meaning or purpose, where the search for kicks could only lead to physical and mental decay.

This came home to me forcefully one day when my friend Glen and I had been stopped by the police for dangerous driving. We were annoyed – getting lectured by the police didn't fit in with our need for respect – so we had a few more beers in Glen's apartment, then went out for a walk. Before we left, I saw him slip a nine-millimetre service pistol in his pocket. In the yard behind the building we came across an old white tramp sitting in the shade of a tree and drinking methylated spirits. Suddenly I saw what I could become, and my fury erupted.

"Give me the gun!" I snapped, and walked up to the old man. I took off the safety catch and placed the muzzle against his head.

"Are you ready to die?" I asked him. "You're a disgrace to humanity!"

The old man looked at up at me with bloodshot eyes and pleaded for his life; Glen was laughing and shouting, "Pop him in the head, just pop him!"

"You're a piece of rubbish!" I shouted, and started to squeeze the trigger.

Just then a nearby window opened and a woman leaned out. "What do you think you're doing?" she called.

I put the gun back in my pocket, leaned over the old tramp and put my mouth close to his ear.

"I'm coming back to kill you," I said, and we walked away.

As my anger subsided I wondered what made me behave like that. I had come close to shooting a man

I didn't even know. I think it was a complicated response to the fact that I hated my life; I hated the guilt and remorse that stalked me, and the pointless drinking bouts that were my only way of keeping those thoughts away; and I hated the fact that I had been programmed to channel tension and fear into anger, and anger into violence.

Violence in the townships

Meanwhile, the South Africa of my childhood was changing. Resistance to apartheid had been growing ever since the mid-1970s, when conditions for the blacks became even more oppressive. In 1976 an initially peaceful demonstration against the Bantu Education Act (making the use of Afrikaans compulsory in black schools) was held by hundreds of schoolchildren in Soweto. The police responded with tear gas and gunfire, provoking a riot that went on for days and left hundreds dead. It was a landmark for black resistance; afterwards many young blacks joined MK (*Umkhonto we Sizwe*, the armed wing of the banned African National Congress) and trained as guerrillas – they believed that the only way to achieve change was through a "people's war", involving the whole country in the fight against apartheid.

There followed a period of increasing unrest, with wildcat strikes, especially in the mining industry, as blacks protested about low wages and discriminatory labour laws. The ANC ran a campaign of sabotage, bombing police stations, power installations and, in 1983, the headquarters of the South African Air Force in Pretoria. Throughout the early

1980s there were hundreds of arrests and many organisations were banned in an effort to contain these attacks.

At the same time there were some signs of a change of stance in the South African government, which was faced with international disapproval of apartheid, resulting in trade and investment sanctions. President P W Botha proposed a power-sharing scheme, which was agreed in a whites-only referendum. It made a token distribution of political power between whites, coloureds and Indians, in the proportions 4:2:1 – so that the whites would retain their majority rule.

By the mid-1980s there was conflict in the townships, as people rioted, burned government buildings and tried to destroy the apartheid administration. This was no longer blacks attacking whites; there were attacks on the homes of black policemen and town councillors, who were seen as "collaborators" with the system. There were other elements in the "black-on-black" violence, too. There were political conflicts between the left-wing Xhosa-based ANC and the right-wing Zulu-dominated Inkatha; there were also tribal enmities, gang warfare and fights between the township-dwellers and the migrant workers crowded into huge hostels nearby.

Over the next five years the necessity for real change and the eventual dismantling of apartheid became inevitable, but even as this was happening the government struggled to keep control of the situation. A national State of Emergency was declared; the police were given sweeping new powers to detain people indefinitely without charge; strict TV, radio and press censorship was imposed; and 5,000 troops were deployed in the townships to quell resistance. In 1984 Archbishop Tutu commented that on the roads leading into the townships there were often road-blocks manned by the army in routine police operations. "When you use the army in this fashion," he said, "who is the enemy?"

It was against this background that I was called up, from 1982 onwards, for my service in the annual military camps.

CHAPTER (9)

Back into Action

I HAD MIXED FEELINGS about being recalled to military service. In many ways I had enjoyed my time in the Paras – the pride in our achievements, the sense of purpose, the excitement and the camaraderie – but it had been two whole years quite unlike any others, focused entirely on a special way of life and separate from everything else. Now it was with a feeling of dread that I opened the registered letter bearing my registration number and inviting me to report to 3 Parachute Battalion, the Civilian Force Unit. It interrupted the freedom of my comfortable civilian life, and returned me to the regimented hardships of the military.

Before we could be deployed in active service, of course, we had to retrain – partly to refresh our memories on how to handle weapons, and partly to get us back up to the kind of physical fitness required for parachuting. When I did my Section-Leader training I had been taught how to use a light machine gun (which was actually a heavy beast), and now a group of us went out to the shooting range to regain our old skills. We shot round after round for practice, and eventually set the bush veld alight with tracer bullets; we spent the rest of the day and night fighting the fierce bush fire we'd started.

We then had a refresher parachute course, with

five practice jumps. I thought I remembered everything about technique, and I imagined that I'd kept
pretty fit, yet I seemed to land badly and hurt myself
every time. After the fourth jump my friend Robbie
said, "Hey, Johnny, if you go on like this you're going
to kill yourself on the last one." Just to add to our
troubles, on the final jump we had to carry the light
machine gun, first-line ammunition, water and
rations – and it was at night.

As I stepped out of the plane into the moonlight I
knew I'd made a good exit. I could hear Malcolm and
Robbie ahead of me shouting to each other, then the
thuds and gasps as they landed heavily in the darkness – at night it was always hard to tell exactly when
you were going to hit the ground. I made a near-per-
fect landing, released my equipment and harness,
and called out to Malcolm, "Are you OK?" There was
no answer, so I shouted, "Robbie, come and help, I
think Malcolm's hurt."

"I can't help," he called back. "I think I've broken
my leg!"

I made my way over to Malcolm (who had a slight
concussion) and then back to Robbie. I had the last
laugh as he came back to the unit a few days later
with a huge white plaster cast on his leg.

After our training we were ready to be deployed
once again, but this time we didn't have to travel
across the border – now the war had come to us, and
was being fought inside our own country. The townships were burning – Soweto, New Brighton,
Khayelitsha and Alexandria – and it was our job to try
to contain a movement that was gathering momen-

tum all the time. Sometimes we were trying to keep the blacks out of the white suburbs, and sometimes we were inside the townships trying to quell riots and keep rival factions apart.

Over the next few years I alternated between life at home – where I worked, fought, drank and constantly looked for some kind of excitement and satisfaction – and life at the annual camp, where I retrained and went out with my rifle to protect my country. It should have given me the excitement I craved, but instead of shooting enemy soldiers I was being told to fire at black civilians. It was hard to take a pride in that.

At the height of the violence in Guguletu and the adjoining KTC townships outside Cape Town, I was deployed with three companies of 3 Para Battalion for a three-month camp. We patrolled the streets in armoured vehicles, trying to separate the ANC supporters from the *Witdoekers* (who backed the government). The township houses were mostly two-roomed, brick-built homes, but in the squatter camp alongside there were hundreds of shanties constructed of corrugated iron, wood and plastic sheeting. Once a fire was started they were soon all ablaze, and hundreds of them were completely destroyed. We were positioned between the opposing forces, challenged by armed activists and freedom fighters from all walks of life, with the homeless begging us to help them and the workers who had jobs in Cape Town demanding that we escort them to work in safety.

Even though the media were censored in South Africa, there was world-wide television coverage, and the international community probably knew more about what went on in the townships than most South Africans did. Camera crews filmed us guarding government buildings as petrol bombs were thrown at us – white soldiers unpopular with both sides – standing our ground and trying to keep the peace. We had a military lawyer who had briefed us about the problems of policing the townships, and the dangers of responding to provocation. Sometimes African women would run ahead of our vehicles as we patrolled and lift their blouses and skirts; once the police questioned some *troeps* from our unit because they had beaten up several youths who had been standing in the road giving us Black Power salutes. We later heard that the boys had been bribed by some foreign photographers to taunt us, so that they could record the response.

We patrolled in our open vehicles day and night, in the rain and the cold. At night we were equipped with a searchlight and a radio, and we stopped regularly to report our position. We were in a township in our own country, but we were in just as much danger from snipers as we had been on the battlefield. My mate Ross and I were allocated to the police as guards, riding on the Caspirs that were once operational against SWAPO. Now we were using them as anti-riot vehicles, souped up by the mechanics to give them more power.

One day our wheels got stuck in a muddy area between the houses, and we were sitting on the vehicle, reminiscing with an ex-Koevoet operator about the bush war. We didn't notice the people moving to surround us until the officer shouted, "Dismount and form all-round defence!" Then we realised that a hostile mob had gathered, and they started pelting us with stones. I fastened my riot helmet tightly and rolled down my sleeves to absorb the impact of the rocks, and jumped down to face the crowd. We didn't have much armament: the police had pump-action shotguns and side arms, and Ross and I had automatic rifles and five full magazines with 175 rounds each.

By now there were around 800 people in the crowd, and our radio contact with HQ told us to stand by, as the police helicopter and other vehicles in the area were coming to help. Just then I noticed a man in the distance pointing what looked like a weapon at me. I placed my rifle sights at 500 metres and levelled out for the shot. The group around him dispersed and he raised both hands in the air, showing me the hammer he had been pretending was a weapon. He had narrowly escaped being killed.

Eventually our driver managed to bounce the Caspir out of the mud and we made a hasty getaway, glad of the extra power in our engine. As we roared off, our bumper caught a wooden fence and we brought the whole lot down, to shouts of anger from the crowd.

We dealt with many disturbances like this in the volatile areas around Cape Town, including petrol bombings and car and house fires. These attacks often targeted individuals, but the crime I hated most was necklacing. This was the punishment chosen by illegal kangaroo courts, where informers were found guilty of selling information to the police. The victims would be forced to drink petrol, then their hands would be tied behind their backs and a car tyre stuffed with newspaper was placed over their heads and set alight. As the rubber tyre melted, the wire supports inside would be exposed and hang round the victim's neck – hence the necklace. Then the body would explode as the petrol ignited. It was a hideous form of public execution, performed to instil fear in the non-political inhabitants of the townships.

We even saw children playing at necklacing – they had watched these executions and made them part of their games. Once we were able to break up a crowd of young men by firing over their heads, and in the centre of the group we found a stranger who was about to be executed because he refused to swear allegiance to their particular party.

Many of the police were fervent supporters of Eugene Terre' blanche – known in Afrikaans as *Oom* (uncle) – the extreme militant right-wing leader. He believed that only force would control the townships. When we were called to a disturbance at a high school in Wynburg, we took in nine Caspirs to guard the police. The riot police detonated tear-gas canisters in a crowd of young coloured students, and allowed their dogs to savage them as they tried to get away. When the teachers questioned the actions of the police they were beaten with *sjamboks* and night-stick batons. It wasn't surprising that such shows of force were met with ever-increasing violence in return. At the St James Church in Cape Town nine believers died when Pan African Congress guerrillas attacked with assault rifles and hand grenades during a church service. Terrorism was springing up everywhere.

On another occasion we were called out to the University of Cape Town, where sympathetic white students were demonstrating. Members of the Students' Union were on the rampage, breaking windows and knocking over the bins, and we drove up in our armoured vehicles and stopped in De Waal Drive, opposite the university buildings. I hoped we wouldn't have to go into action: my sister was a student at the university, studying dietetics, and here was I, parked outside, waiting to attack. I was very glad when the order came to stand down.

I never knew exactly how the authorities allocated reservists to these annual camps; it all seemed pretty random. Usually you found yourself with a new stick of men each time. However, by some strange coincidence there was one constant figure in my camps: at every one I attended I would find Sean, another Bat whom I first met when I was doing my military service. Sean was a real character, a Christian who wasn't ashamed to talk about his faith. This was unusual in the army, where most people avoided admitting to anything that would mark them out as different from their mates. Religion wasn't something most people wanted to talk about, and if anything it was thought of as a bit soft, but Sean just didn't fit into anyone's stereotypes. His faith didn't make him lose any of his toughness and aggression, and he was respected for his ability as a professional soldier. He was also a black belt in karate, so he wasn't someone you would pick a fight with!

Over the years Sean and I had trained together on the LMG (light machine gun), helped newly qualified Puma pilots with ground deployment and hot extractions, and patrolled the townships night after night in dangerous situations. One night we were driving fast through a burning street, and I heard him shout, "In Jesus' name, I take authority over you, Devil!" I put my rifle into the firing position and shouted, "Where? Where?", thinking he was talking about a real physical threat. He said it was the power of evil he was shouting at, the spiritual forces that incited people to hate and kill each other. From anyone else it might have sounded crazy, but not from Sean. I knew he was such a normal guy. We fought side by side and knew we could rely on each other. It was just that I believed that my protection was my weapon, and Sean believed that his protection was his God. I envied him because he really didn't seem to be afraid of anything; he was always prepared to die.

He never minded the compulsory church parades the army forced on us; I suppose they made more sense to him than they did to me. Then one afternoon the minister didn't pitch up for the service, and Sean offered to lead it. It was weird, seeing my mate standing up there reading the Bible in front of all the guys, as if it was perfectly normal. Then something happened that wasn't normal at all. He finished up by praying for anyone who was sick, and there was one *troep* there who had been in Delta Company with me. I knew he was deaf – he had been wounded in a battle and the bomb blast had deafened him. Sean put his hands on him and prayed, and the guy looked up in amazement: he could hear. He had been healed. It hadn't really occurred to me before that things like that could happen nowadays – though I'd sat in church for long enough as a child to know all the Bible stories about healing. It made me start thinking that Sean really did have something special about him, and that it might be something I ought to get into. I think I knew then, deep in my heart, that one day I would end up serving God. I just wasn't ready to think about it.

Civilian life

In 1986 I went to Speskops (Special Forces HQ) in Pretoria to enquire about applying for the Recce course again, but by the time the next selection came round I had lost interest. I was also approached by the CCB (Civil Corporation Bureau), a sort of state-sponsored Secret Service extension of the SADF. Some of my friends had joined them, carrying out political assassinations so that the military could deny any involvement. While I was on camp these military careers always seemed more attractive, but when I got back to civilian life I forgot about them. Once home and enjoying my freedom, I didn't want to be regimented by army discipline any more.

So back I went each time to the old routines of drinking and fighting, every year getting more bored with the short-lived excitements available from antagonising other drinkers and provoking fist fights. The slightest thing was worth a fight. One night at a party I got up to dance with my girlfriend, and when we got back to our table a young guy was sitting in my chair. I started off politely:

"Excuse me, you're sitting in my seat."

"It's my party," he replied, "and I'll sit where I want."

"That's fine, but not in my chair," I said, and pulled him out of the seat by the scruff of his neck. He moved away as I sat down, then flew across the table, punching at me. My girlfriend was pulling me down by my sweater, saying, "Please don't fight," but I just looked at her in amazement. How could you not fight when someone was attacking you? One of my friends came in on my side, and a couple of his on the other, and I got the guy in an expert armlock round the neck. I applied enough pressure to start choking him and said, "I'll go all the way, friend!" In the end we were chased off by about 30 men and finished up having a free-for-all in the road until a truce was called.

Part of my suppressed anger and desperation was born out of a kind of depression. More and more, as I looked around me, I seemed to see death. There were plenty of young men like me around, all responding in the same way to the partying and drinking, by getting aggressive and starting fights. One night I took a gun from one guy who was looking dangerously drunk, and gave it back to him later when I thought he had sobered up a bit. He took it from me and got into his car to drive home. Later I heard that he had driven over an embankment and been killed. He left a wife and young children. Another childhood friend of mine had joined the ParaBats and was still in training. One night he took a handgun illegally brought into barracks by one of his mates, and shot himself in the head. It all seemed so pointless. There was enough killing on the battlefield, where it couldn't be avoided – why would people kill themselves carelessly by drink-driving, or intentionally by committing suicide?

Suddenly life seemed to be increasingly fragile. It could be wiped out in a moment, through thoughtlessness or by accident. Every time I left a military camp, I left behind scenes of violence and hatred in the black townships. Back in the cities it should have been peaceful and safe, but everywhere I looked I saw accidents on the roads or building sites, people who had chosen to take their own lives or who were too despairing to care whether they lived or died. Somehow, when I saw deaths in civilian life, I felt even more vulnerable. As a soldier I knew how to defend myself, by my training, my ability to handle a weapon, by the state of constant alert tension that was life on the battlefield. As a civilian I felt as if death could catch up with me anywhere, while I was working or crossing the street, and I had nothing to protect me.

I had survived years of war, in the bush veldt of South West Africa and Angola, and in the townships of South Africa. I had not died in those battles, but now I found I didn't know how to live. I still wanted to survive, but it seemed that death was all around me. What was the point of living like this?

CHAPTER (10)

A Different Life

FOR MOST OF THOSE YEARS after my demobilisation
I was living alone or with friends: during my apprenticeship my parents had moved to the Eastern Cape
region to start their own business. As far as they were
concerned, I was over 21, legally of age and independent, with a good job. I could manage without them.
I used to say that I wouldn't leave home, so home left
me! First I lived with some friends, but later I moved
in with my girlfriend, much to the disapproval of my
mother and grandmother. I was young and free to
live the way I wanted, and I certainly wasn't going to
acknowledge that I felt lost and alone, or that I
missed the security, support and boundaries that
family life gave me.

By 1987 I decided I'd had enough of Johannesburg.
Terrorism was on the increase and bombs outside
public buildings were frequent. I was working in the
Rand International Hotel when a car bomb was detonated just down the street at the Witwatersrand
Command of the SADF. The blast was tremendous,
and I instinctively dropped to the ground as windows
shattered all along the street. The huge plate-glass
window beside me flexed in and out, but fortunately
it didn't break. When I climbed cautiously to my feet
and looked out, there was dust and debris everywhere.
Bodies were scattered across the road, mangled cars

had been thrown onto the pavements, and several buildings were badly damaged. I was sickened by the waste of life, and depressed at the ease with which it could be snatched away. It brought home to me the pointlessness of my own life, and I decided I was bored of partying and fighting. I wanted something better – even if that meant living with my parents. I made my way to Uitenhage, where they were living, and started a small plumbing business of my own.

For a while things seemed to improve. Running my own business kept me busy and gave me a sense of purpose and responsibility, and for a while I even took an interest in Christianity. I met a Christian who tried to teach me and give me some help, but he had problems of his own to work out, and I knew he couldn't help me with mine. He seemed to think that we could work together – that is, I would work at my plumbing business, and he would live off the proceeds. That didn't seem to me to be a particularly good deal, so I refused his kind offer.

I think I knew, deep down, that Jesus could be the answer to my emptiness, but I still wasn't ready to find out. I kept coming across people who talked about God, and I met Sean at every military camp, but I hadn't actually encountered Jesus for myself. I couldn't believe that God could love me, because I had done so many terrible things. Anyway, I had an idea that if ever I got serious about Christianity, I would have to change my wild ways, and I didn't think I could manage to live a different kind of life.

Even in Uitenhage I was still drinking too much and smoking a lot of *dagga* (cannabis) – thank God I never had anything to do with hard drugs or needles – and I often ended up spending the warm South African nights sleeping on the pavement. In the morning I would stumble to my feet, find the keys to my motorbike, and drive to work. Living with my parents had done nothing to help me learn some self-discipline. I was still out of control, ruled by the guilt and fear that drove me to seek the same futile ways of escape. I realised that I had travelled 1,000 kilometres only to find myself back in the same old environment. No matter how far I ran, I couldn't run away from myself.

I went back to Johannesburg and moved back in with my girlfriend. I accepted that this was just the way things were going to be, drinking in the same bars, getting into fights, going to work to earn some money for more drink and smoke. Life was pointless, and I was resigned; one day I would pick a fight with the wrong guy, or step into the road at the wrong moment, or my reflexes wouldn't be quite fast enough at the next military camp, and that would be the end of me – my life would be snuffed out.

One night I was sitting at home flicking between the TV channels. There was nothing on that I wanted to watch, and when I found myself gazing blankly at the test card, I was suddenly filled with irritation. I threw the remote control at the screen, furious that there was nothing on TV to distract me from my depression. That was when God spoke to me.

"What would happen if you died today?" The thought came into my head as clearly as if someone in the room had spoken.

"I don't care," I answered. "I don't care if I die."

Then I sat up, realising that it wasn't true. "I *do* care," I said. "That's what I've been trying to escape. God, I do care."

I suddenly saw that it was death I had been running away from, in war and in civilian life. People had died all around me and I didn't want to die. It was a great turning-point for me, realising that I did care. I wanted to live.

The next step was up to God, and he took it. I was working with a young electrician called Clint, and one day he said to me, "I'm a Christian now. I've received Jesus as my saviour." I laughed at him.

"You?" I said. "You're talking rubbish, man. You don't even know Jesus. You're such a bad guy, Jesus could never forgive you for some of the things you've done."

"Well, it's true," said Clint. "I'm a believer now."

"No way," I said. "I know believers. Believers always have a Bible. Where's your Bible?"

He went to his bag and brought out the biggest Bible I've ever seen – big enough to choke a dinosaur! I had to agree that he could be a believer with a Bible like that. Then he said, "Why don't you come to church with me, and see what it's like?" I wasn't keen, but I agreed to go with him on Sunday to Rhema Church. They were having a special service which was being televised. Well, Rhema wasn't like any church I'd ever been to. No cross, no genuflecting, no organ – but a big brass band playing loud music and thousands of people. And there at the door was my friend

Sean, saying, "Hey, Johnny, I've been waiting for you. I've saved you a place next to us at the front."

"Oh no," I said. "There are cameras over there. This stuff's being shown on national television. What if my mates see me?" They took no notice and led me off to their seats – Clint and his girlfriend, and Sean and his girlfriend, and me sitting there in the middle.

It was a good service, and the preacher talked about accepting Jesus in a way I'd never heard before – or perhaps I'd never been ready to listen. Now I felt a great conviction that I wanted God to take over my life – I certainly wasn't doing much good running it myself. Everything he said answered the things I had been thinking. Jesus had died for me, so that I didn't have to die. Jesus had taken my sins to himself so that I could escape from the load of guilt I'd been carrying. I could have a new life if I wanted it. The preacher led us in prayer, and then asked us to raise our hand if we wanted to accept Jesus, and I raised mine. I thought "What am I doing?" and I pulled it down, but it went straight back up. Then I heard him say, "God bless you, I see that hand," and I knew that one other person, at least, knew that I had committed myself to Jesus. Still, everyone else had their heads bowed in prayer, so that was OK.

Then he said, "Right, if you've put your hand up, then stand up." I was thinking, "Oh, no, no." But the preacher went on, "Jesus died on the cross for you in public, so you can receive him in public." I didn't want to do it, but when he said, "Come forward," I went forward and knelt with the others in front of everyone. I was filled with a tremendous sense of peace.

It seemed that ever since I entered the army I had been fighting for my life. I had fought physically against well-armed enemies on the field of battle, only to find in the years that followed that I had no idea how to live the life that was left to me, emotionally or spiritually. Ever since those days I had been walking around like a zombie, physically alive but spiritually dead. Filled with guilt and remorse, I had almost accepted that death was the only way out. But now I had been offered the most wonderful opportunity. Jesus had borne the penalty for all the things I had done, and taken all my guilt on his shoulders. He had died for me, so that I might live, and he was offering to fill me with his Spirit and give me new life. There were tears in my eyes, because I knew that the fight was over at last, and I was staying alive for ever. I was in God's presence and his safe keeping.

A change of direction

When I was conscripted at the age of 17 I became a soldier straight away, but it took long months of training before I could fight like one. I gave my life to Jesus at the age of 27, accepted his forgiveness and became a Christian, but it took a long time before I learned to behave like one. I knew that if I wanted to serve God I had to make my life conform to my convictions, and try to live according to his law, but it didn't come easily to me. You aren't a sinner one day and a saint the next. What God had to do with me was a process, and sometimes it was a painful one.

Just around the time I made my commitment, a friend asked me if I would be best man at his wedding. The stag night was held at the local tennis club, and we had a barbecue with about 40 guys drinking huge amounts of alcohol. Then my brother said, "Can you help us move these tables, John? We need to make space for the strippers." I hadn't known they were coming. I moved the furniture and then stood at one side as the two girls danced seductively in front of us. They made it clear that they were available, and I pleaded with my friend not to sleep with them, because I knew he would regret it later.

We'd been friends a long time, since we were at technical college together, and we had been to plenty of parties like this. I used to enjoy them. I could hardly believe that my attitude had changed so much: one girl passed close by, flashing her bare breasts at me, and I just looked away. I decided it was time for me to leave, so I moved off towards the open door and went outside, but God hadn't finished with the lesson he wanted to teach me. My car was on the other side of town, so I hitched a lift in a left-hand drive American limo. As soon as I got into the car I realised my mistake – the driver was drunk. He drove fairly slowly to start with, until I noticed that he was falling asleep, and shouted to wake him up. Then he started driving like a maniac at breakneck speed, and I had to grab the wheel to avoid hitting some oil drums at the side of the road. It was only as I thanked him for the lift and got out of the car that I remembered how often I had driven in a similar state, without a thought for my own or my passenger's safety. I asked God's forgiveness as I went to collect my car.

Ten minutes later I was offering a lift to another

young hitch-hiker, and I started telling him about what had happened, and how my life had been changed by God. As I dropped him off at his destination I saw that there were tears in his eyes.

"Is everything OK?" I asked.

"My wife's having an affair," he answered. "I've got a gun and I was going to kill her tonight. But I know God doesn't want me to do it."

We prayed together and I took the rounds out of his firearm; then he went home to try to sort out his relationship. I was stunned. I could hardly believe God's timing – that within such a short time he would use me to reach another person at such a critical moment. Was this what being a Christian was like?

I went to Sean and asked him.

"That's right, Johnny," he said. "Life's never boring when you're doing God's will!"

"How do I do God's will?" I asked. "How do I know what he wants me to do?"

"Just look around," he said. "And when you find something that's God's work, do it with all your might."

What I saw, when I looked around, was the Rhema Street Ministry. Groups from the church would go out into the streets of Johannesburg, preaching and evangelising, and I knew I wanted to be part of that. We used to meet at the church on a Saturday morning for prayer, and then we would go out into the town centre. Because it was a shopping district, with some tower blocks of flats nearby, we weren't allowed to use a public address system, but we had live music, which attracted a crowd. Then we

would preach and give short testimonies, and someone would invite people to give their hearts to the
Lord. It was amazing – hundreds of people would
come forward, wanting to know more about Jesus. I
had never imagined that there was a such a hunger
for the love of God.

Then one day our evangelist, Peter Rahme, asked
me to give my testimony. I had never done any public
speaking, but I stood up and started to talk about
what God had done in my life, with an interpreter
standing beside me, translating my words into Zulu.
It was a strange experience – the words just flowed
out as I spoke from my heart. At one point the interpreter was speaking at great length and I turned to
see who was giving him all this to say, and was surprised to realise it was me – I felt, literally, "beside
myself".

One of the outstanding things about the ministry
was the way it reached out to both black and white
alike, without any discrimination. It was a lesson I
was having to learn slowly myself. I had never
thought of myself as a racist, but I suppose that growing up in South Africa's culture of apartheid had set
certain attitudes in my mind. God was changing
those.

One day we went visiting in the local government
hospital. I had been there before, many years ago,
when my grandmother was having an eye operation,
so I thought I knew what to expect: white people
being cared for by white staff. However, times had
changed, and both the patients and staff were black.
I saw one of our group sitting with a group of little

black children, with his arm around one and another on his lap, as he told them stories about Jesus. I felt a surge of confused anger rise up in me, and as usual had a violent impulse to hit him. What did he think he was doing? Then I recognised the source of my irritation. He had crossed the line of my prejudice by being affectionate to black children – little innocent children who had done nothing wrong. That was when I saw how much work God needed to do in me. He had removed my guilt, but he also had to remove my anger and my prejudice. I needed my mind as well as my heart to be renewed.

The moment I recognised this, I lifted the thought to God in prayer: "Lord, please give me a heart for all your people, black and white." The answer was immediate. I walked into the next ward and saw an old black man who was weeping with pain. Suddenly my heart was filled with compassion. I put my arms round him and prayed with him, and kissed him on the head. Then I knew that I could be a channel for the love of Jesus, and that to God it doesn't matter whether you are male or female, rich or poor, white or black. His love enfolds us all.

All this time South African politics had been grinding their slow way towards the ending of the apartheid system. The ban on the ANC had been lifted and both Walter Sisulu and Nelson Mandela had been released from prison; in 1990 King Goodwill Zilintweni, king of the Zulus, was invited to sign a Peace Accord at a Johannesburg hotel. That Saturday morning we were preaching on the street when we saw people running towards us in panic. Behind them 800 Zulu men dressed as *impi* (warriors) were running, armed with traditional weapons. They were led by *indunas* (chiefs) coming to pay homage to their king, but they looked extremely warlike and threatening, and in the volatile Johannesburg of those days, anything could happen. Someone shouted, "They are IFP!" – Inkatha Freedom Party – which caused more panic. Any kind of political confrontation between the black political parties could end in violence. We placed our black brothers in the centre of our group for protection, and joined in prayer, though as the warriors passed, every one of us expected to be struck by a fighting stick. We were relieved when the demonstration passed peacefully, and we continued to pray for peace for the rest of the day.

In those days I often preached about our need for forgiveness for the years of apartheid. In South Africa the whites had had a good, easy life for many years, but we had to face up to the fact that apartheid was an evil injustice in our midst. Our society needed to change. In the same way, we have to face up to the realities in our personal lives. We may have a good material life, we may go through the motions of civilised living, but we have to face up to our own spiritual darkness. Every one of us falls short of the holiness of God, and we need to ask his forgiveness and his help in changing our lives.

CHAPTER 11

Christians in Training

ALL THE TIME I WAS WORKING with the street ministry I saw older, more mature Christians doing God's work with amazing power. Peter Rahme, our evangelist, had a great gift for reaching out to people. I once saw him take a nine-millimetre handgun from a gangster who had come into church with a group of his friends. "You have respect out on the street," he said. "This is God's church and I ask you to respect it when you come in."

Once when he was preaching, one of these young guys said, "This is rubbish."

Peter replied, "Shall I prove to you that my Jesus is more powerful than your religion?" He took the man by the hand, said, "My friend, I love you," and kissed him. Then he said, "Now you kiss me."

The guy was really embarrassed. He said, "I can't."

"So my Jesus is more powerful, because he gives me the power to love you, and the courage to be willing to show it."

Peter could get alongside anyone. One day we were preaching in a shopping arcade when a group of young Zulu dancers came by, beating animal-skin drums and blowing whistles. The music they were making had a beat like the heart of Africa, and Peter started dancing to it. Soon we were all dancing, joining in with the Zulu dancers, and the crowd joined in with us. We were praising God and dancing for the Lord like David did at the Temple, and the people were amazed to see that white men could be as joyful and uninhibited as the Africans. When the drums finally stopped beating and the dancers stood still, we witnessed to the crowd. Over 500 people responded to our message of joy and love.

I knew that if my preaching was to have that kind of authenticity it had to come from my heart, but I also needed to have a good understanding of what the Bible says. "Wisdom is supreme; therefore get wisdom. Though it cost all you have, get understanding" (Proverbs 4:7). I wanted a closer walk with God, and I wanted to understand what he was saying to me through his word. I began to think about enrolling at Bible college, so that I could get the kind of understanding I needed. I didn't know what plans God had for my life; I just wanted to learn more about Jesus.

It was around then that an American evangelist called James Roberson came to preach at Rhema Church. His message was that God needed messengers to change lives, and he called for a commitment from those who were willing to lay down their life and follow the Lord in full-time ministry. I had never thought about such a thing – I was only a plumber, with not much education – but suddenly I knew that God was speaking to me once more. He wanted me to be willing to work for him and do his will, and I knew that whatever he had in mind for me, I wanted to do

A fourteen-day road trip involving eating and sleeping in the bush.

On the road with Jesus Alive Ministries: these conditions persisted for thousands of kilometres.

John in Goma, Zaire, on radio duty in 1994.

The refugee children in the Goma camp were starting to respond.

Goma camp, after a meal had been served: thousands of children can make quite a mess.

John and team with their aircraft at Goma Airport after a supplies run.

Johannesburg, 2000: the precious ladies who served at The Mission, distributing food to the homeless.

Young homeless men enjoying a hot meal outside The Mission.

Young men whom we took in and discipled at the Mission Life Centre, the farm outside Johannesburg.

Tracy Dudlu with children from the streets of Hillbrow, Yeoville and Johannesburg. These children are being cared for, educated, fed, clothed and loved.

At a township church in 2003. Note the newspaper covering the corrugated iron wall.

Each year, Mission Link International raises money for Blankets for Africa, for use by the homeless, many of whom are HIV victims. Blankets are essential during the winter months of June, July and August. These blankets are used for sleeping, as a coat, and for carrying babies on backs.

Uganda crusade: platform built of forest timber.

OFFICIAL FINISH TIME 05:03:49 **FLORA LONDON MARATHON 2003**

John has completed three London marathons.

John and Tara with Jade, Liam and Dylan in Bristol, UK, 2003.

it, with all my heart. I went forward and knelt at the altar with a crowd of other young people. Little did I know that my future wife was on her knees at the other side of the altar, offering her life to Jesus as I was offering mine.

In 1990 I enrolled at Rhema Bible Training Centre for the two-year ministerial course; I was part of the evening class, and attended lectures and did my studying in the evenings after I had finished work. It was hard work but I didn't mind; I knew I had a lot to learn. I first met Tara when I was standing in line waiting to register at Rhema. A friend had already told me about her; he said that his wife knew a young hairstylist who was a Christian, and they were sure we would get on. When I heard this gorgeous young woman introduce herself to the dean of the college as a hairdresser, I knew it had to be her. When I spoke to her it was clear that these matchmakers had already been at work: she said, "I know who you are; your blue eyes gave you away!"

I wasn't prepared for Tara's forthrightness; on Valentine's Day she asked me out for a meal. At first I hesitated, saying it would be late by the time we finished our evening class, and the restaurant would be sure to be crowded. In the end I agreed, and was astounded when I realised that she had already reserved our table! I was impressed.

We had only been going out for a couple of months when we knew we wanted to spend the rest of our lives together, but we had to be sure it was God's will. We prayed about it at the end of a church service, and asked the pastor if we could join his three-month marriage preparation course. He talked to us both, and then said that in our case he recommended a six-month course of weekly counselling sessions! We understood. We were both relatively new Christians, and we were both still learning how to live in God's will. We needed to be very sure of our commitment to each other and to understand the meaning of Christian marriage.

I especially had a lot to learn. I was still quick to get angry, and my lightning reflexes often responded with violence before I had time to think. When I went into my evening Bible class, it seemed that every young man there would slap me on the back in greeting. My desk was at the front of the class, and one evening as we arrived for our time of praise and worship, two heavy hands descended on my back. I spun round, grabbed the friendly guy by the neck and kicked his legs out from under him. The rest of the class came to his rescue and said, "John, what are you doing?"

I came to my senses and felt very embarrassed. "Just trying to praise the Lord in my own way," I muttered.

Another time I watched a young man greet Tara with what I thought was an unnecessarily long hug. I followed him to the toilets and threatened him: "If you ever touch Tara again, I'll hurt you!" God spoke to me after that, and said, "Deal with your anger." I realised that this was not how Christians should behave, but I had many long years of habit to shake off.

I knew I needed to change, but I didn't know how. I just relied on God to show me the way in his good time. I was helped by so many people; by Peter Rahme, by Tara, and by other friends who came at just the right moment to give me a word of guidance. One of my Bible-school friends had served in the Special Forces Medics in the Ops Area, and one day as we talked over old times I got out my military photo album. It didn't just have photos in it; it also contained mementoes of those days, like the Angolan money I had taken off my first kill.

"It's a good album, John," he said, "but you're still proud of those achievements. They belong to your old lifestyle. They don't belong in the life you're living now."

I might not have listened to anyone else challenging me about my past, but I knew he understood. He grew up in the same tough Johannesburg suburb as me; he went to the same school, and he had been in the bush war. He knew what all those things meant. "I do want to be free of my past," I told him. "I don't need pictures to remind me of the horrors of those days."

That night I burned the album and everything in it. It was only as the flames devoured the last scraps of paper that I realised what I had done, and my heart was broken. I wept as I had never wept before, as I realised that I had finally let go of the memories that haunted me. My old life had been destroyed, and now God was able to start a fresh work in me. I could face the future without looking back all the time.

Later on I was often able to help other ex-combat soldiers to do the same thing, burning the horrific pictures they had kept for years, and setting them free in the forgiveness of Jesus.

I was always busy, going to work each day, and studying at Bible college each evening. At weekends I went out with the street ministry and saw God's power in action. It was all I needed to keep focused on my purpose: to study and learn more about him, so that I could be useful in his ministry. God gave me some wonderful experiences during this time, to encourage me.

One day I went to a Christian bookshop in my lunch hour, and got talking to the shop assistant. He was telling me about a young man he knew who was troubled by his past life, and how this seemed to hold him back from making a full commitment to Jesus. Two African women came into the shop to pay for a Bible, and as we all talked together I began to tell them something of my story, and how God had saved me from the guilt of my own experiences. There followed something that some people would call a coincidence, but I have come to see as a God-incident. The young man we had been discussing came into the shop, just as I was talking about how I had left my old life behind. Then the shop assistant began speaking about the power of God and the baptism of the Holy Spirit, and I could feel that the Spirit of God was moving among us. As I prayed with the young man, he fell backwards, struck down by the awesome power of God. When he stood up he was praising God in another language, just as people did in the Bible. "All of them were filled with the Holy Spirit and began to speak in other tongues as the Spirit enabled them" (Acts 2:4).

Then the assistant turned to me, and it seemed to

me that his face had changed – he looked suddenly older and filled with authority. He started speaking about me and my life, sounding like an Old Testament prophet:

"God will raise you up and use you mightily among the nations. He will guide and lead you, and take you beyond your own understanding. His Spirit will rest on you, and you will open doors that no man can close, if you learn to trust in him alone."

I didn't understand everything he said, but I had faith that God would make his words come true. I believed in the words of the Bible: "Trust in the Lord with all your heart and lean not on your own understanding; in all your ways acknowledge him, and he will make your paths straight" (Proverbs 3:5,6).

I was beginning to get a glimmer of light about what God had in store for me. I remembered Sean saying to me that if I wanted to work for God, I should turn my hand to whatever I saw, and do it with all my might. One of the counsellors at Rhema Church asked me why I wanted to join the ministry course, and I found the answer coming to my lips without thinking about it:

"I want to go back and help the people whose lives I once destroyed. I want to be a missionary."

I soon had a chance to experience missions: in our first year at Bible school a group of us were invited to spend a week in outreach in Ulundi, the Zululand provincial capital. We made the six-hour journey in a noisy old bus, and arrived hot, dirty and tired. After freshening up we went out to meet the students at the boarding school. They came from all kinds of backgrounds; many of them came from homes that were supposedly Christian, but their faith was mixed with all kinds of other tribal practices, animism (the belief that there are spirits living in everything, even trees and rocks), ancestor worship and shamanism (witch doctors). Over a period of several days we got to know the pupils and won their trust, telling them something about our lives and hearing about theirs. It was so good to be sharing the love of God with these hungry souls: one evening we prayed with them and many of them received the Holy Spirit into their lives.

We even shared the gospel with the guard on the gate; he didn't speak any English, but I prayed that God would use my limited Zulu to reach him. Somehow we managed to understand each other, and I was able to lead him in a prayer accepting Jesus into his life.

In our second year we went to the landlocked kingdom of Swaziland, to be part of an old-fashioned tent crusade. During the day we were divided into groups, and went out into the suburbs carrying a cross to proclaim that we were followers of Jesus. We had musical instruments, and crowds gathered to hear the music, and stayed to listen to us preaching and praying. We would invite them back to the evening meetings in the tent, where hundreds of people came forward to say that they wanted to welcome the love of God into their lives.

On the last evening some vandals cut the ropes of our huge crusade tent, bringing it to the ground, and we had to transfer the meeting to the school hall. Our evangelist was deeply upset about the loss of the tent, but Tara said to me, "I believe God wants us to go and pray with him." We did so, and the evangelist confessed that his heart had been filled with anger about the incident. Then he spoke a word of prophecy over me and Tara, saying, "From today you will be known as Encouragement!"

That has always been true: even in the hard times we have been able to share the goodness of God, and we have seen wonderful things happen. We have seen miraculous healings, as people in great need have come into our meetings and asked for prayer. Once a man staggered in, desperately holding on to a teddy bear, clearly afraid and unable to understand where he was. We prayed for him and his whole manner changed – it was like seeing a light go on in his mind. He looked around at us in surprise, like someone waking from a dream. When he was able to talk coherently, he told us that he had been addicted to drugs and living as a vagrant for some years. I was amazed to learn that he had once been a medical professional, before he began to sink into depression and despair, which led him into drug abuse and the loss of his home and family. He was freed from his addiction that night, and in the months that followed he began to rebuild his life and return to his career, with one great change: now he trusted Jesus to help and sustain him.

On another occasion we were preaching at the Manzini market when an old man came forward, limping painfully and leaning on a stick. We prayed for him, and he stood up straight and threw away his walking sticks, raising his hands in praise to show what God had done for him.

When the staff at the government hospital in Johannesburg went on strike, the Rhema Bible Training College volunteered to clean the wards and wash the bed linen – we always believed in giving practical help where it was needed. One evening we were taking the garbage bags to the dump in the basement when we found ourselves outside the Intensive Care Unit. We left the bags outside and went in to pray with the nurses, and several of them were filled with the Holy Spirit. Then we quoted the scripture where Jesus said of his followers: "They will place their hands on sick people, and they will get well" (Mark 16:18). We gathered around the bed of a man who had suffered a knife wound; he was unconscious, but as we prayed and laid hands on him he opened his eyes.

It was astounding to see the words of scripture coming alive before our eyes. For most of my life I had thought of religion as something that was shut up in churches, but now I was experiencing the power of God as we reached out and touched lives everywhere we went. The love of Jesus was alive in our world, and we saw conversions and healings and miracles every day. It was so exciting. I said to Tara, "I could do this for the rest of my life." I had found God's plan for me.

CHAPTER  12

Healing
Relationships

WHEN I BECAME A CHRISTIAN, Jesus held a light up to attitudes and prejudices that had been ingrained in me from childhood, and showed me how far they fell short of the way he wanted his children to act towards each other. "'For my thoughts are not your thoughts, neither are your ways my ways,' declares the Lord. 'As the heavens are higher than the earth, so are my ways higher than your ways, and my thoughts than your thoughts'" (Isaiah 55:8,9). Growing up in an apartheid regime had given me an outlook which at the very least did not expect to live or work alongside black people as equals; now all that was changing. I loved and respected the black Christians who worshipped and worked with me in Rhema Church, and I longed to reach out to the many black Africans who had never heard of the redeeming love of Jesus, and bring his new life to them.

However, God doesn't do things by halves, and he wasn't content just with changing my attitude to the people I met. He wanted to check out my relationships with my family, too.

My parents had always taken a fairly easy-going attitude to their children's lives, once we were all adults; they didn't usually criticise or interfere.

However, when I became a Christian, I met with a degree of hostility and confrontation which surprised me. They had put in a huge amount of effort over the years, taking us to Mass and trying to interest us in the Christian faith, yet they were horrified when I told them that I had become a Christian. The problem was that I added, "And I'm leaving the Roman Catholic Church and worshipping at Rhema." Anything I said after that was unimportant.

My mother immediately decided that I had better go and see the Bishop, who was a lifelong friend of my father's – I think she thought that he would sort out my doctrinal problems. "OK," I said. "But only if I can bring my pastor – he knows more theology than I do and he'll be able to help me explain my position better." After that, she let the idea drop. As traditional Catholics, both my parents were shaken by the idea that now I was finally taking an interest in religion, and it was leading me away from what they considered to be the true church. They knew the reputation of Rhema Church and its preaching of the need for everyone to be "born again" spiritually. Among South African Catholics, there was a stigma attached to the term "born again", and they were hurt by it. (On the whole, Roman Catholics don't have an assurance of salvation, because of their belief in Purgatory, where they believe souls are purged from their sins after death.)

My mother was the first to come round. She had always been a major influence on us when we were growing up, and I knew that she knew God, but not as her personal saviour. That kind of personal relationship wasn't preached in the Roman Catholic Church – her faith was in the Creed she recited every Sunday. I was driving past her house one day when I strongly felt the Lord telling me to stop and call in on her.

I found her in the garden, hanging out the washing, and I stood and chatted to her there.

"Mum, I really want to talk to you about God. I know you know *about* him, but he wants you to know him personally, so he can be close to you every day of your life."

To my surprise she agreed, and I led her in the prayer of salvation. It was such a joy to me to see the change in her life after that; she had always been involved with the church, of course, but now she had a new dedication. She took part in a Renewal course, and then took on the new challenge of becoming a course leader. She underwent a full spiritual rebirth, and it was wonderful to see. "If you confess with your mouth, 'Jesus is Lord,' and believe in your heart that God raised him from the dead, you will be saved. For it is with your heart that you believe and are justified, and it is with your mouth that you confess and are saved" (Romans 10:9, 10).

My relationship with my father continued to be uneasy. We rubbed each other up the wrong way; he wouldn't dream of missing his regular attendance at Mass, and he criticised me for not going. I argued that his religion was based on tradition, not conviction. He believed in the saints, and would pray to St Anthony to help him find things; he always fasted on Good Friday, but while he wouldn't dream of eating meat, that didn't stop him tonking back the beers.

One day I asked him what he was planning to do when he retired. "Live," he replied.

"Why not live now?" I asked. He knew where that conversation was heading.

"Don't come here and fight with me in my house, John," he said.

"I'm not fighting with you," I said. "I'm just telling you. There's more to life than just living it. If you really want to live you can only do it through Christ. You can try to live without him, but you can't die without him."

My mother was in the kitchen, and I said to her, "Mum, tell him I'm not fighting with him."

She stuck her head round the door and said, "He's not fighting. You know what you need, Owen Delaney. You need a personal encounter with our Lord. Listen to him."

Dad looked really uncomfortable, and I said, "It's hard to hear these things from your wife and your son." He started looking at me over the top of his glasses – the old-fashioned "stern-father" routine that used to put the fear of God into me when I was a little boy – only it didn't work any more, because I was bigger than him now.

Preparing for marriage

When Tara and I decided to marry, we had to deal with another whole set of problems and antagonism from our families. For a start, I was 27 and Tara was only 19, and my mother thought that she was too young to make such an important lifelong commitment. I pointed out that Tara was very mature for her age – she was a fully qualified hairdresser, and had been independent and earning her living since she was 16. Tara's mother was also nervous about the age difference. We met one day when I called round at her house for a haircut, and I stripped off my T shirt and put a towel round my shoulders in preparation. Her mother took one look at me and said to Tara, "Can I have a word?" She took her out into the hall and said, "Tara, he's a man, not a boy. Are you sure you know what you're doing?"

"It's OK, Mum," Tara said. "I know. And I'm sure."

It helped that both Tara's parents were Christians, and they could see that my commitment to her was genuine. Her father was a quiet man, who just said, "As long as you're happy."

When they realised that after our marriage we intended to be missionaries, both families expressed their concern. Tara's brother had offered to set her up in her own salon, running her own business, and he asked her why she intended to throw away all her prospects. My sister Carol said much the same thing to me, pointing out that I could have made a good living as a plumber. We had to tell them all that we had thought hard about it, and we simply had to follow the path we believed the Lord had set before us. We could never be happy if we knew we had refused to do the work he had asked us to do.

The marriage preparation course we undertook with our pastor helped us both a great deal. He knew our backgrounds, and my history – I had lived with other girlfriends in the past – and he impressed on us that we had to be very sure of our commitment to each other. We needed to understand what marriage as believers really meant, and how we could serve God together. It was very hard, intensive work: we were still working at the day jobs and attending our evening classes at Bible college, and on top of this we had to read books, listen to tapes, and complete challenging assignments. These made us talk about everything – finance, faith, children, discipline, emotions, our attitudes to sex, our experiences of parenting in our childhood, and much more.

We both knew several couples whose marriages had failed, and we were keen to know whether the lengthy questionnaires we had filled out indicated compatibility! Tara was concerned that we should be able to meet each other's emotional needs. I was anxious that my military background, with all the still-untamed anger it had left in me, shouldn't be allowed to spoil this precious and important relationship. We spent many evenings in talking and sharing, and many others in counselling, separately and together, before our pastor agreed that we were ready to take the final step, and commit our lives together to God.

That preparation course was invaluable to us. It developed our relationship rapidly to a much deeper level, so that by the time we married, we knew each other as well as if we had been together for several years. Its value was soon proven: within three months of our wedding we would be working as missionaries out in the field, far away from our families and friends, and totally isolated from any of the support networks that might have helped us over the difficult early ups and downs of married life. It was really good that we had explored so many issues together, and knew our strengths and weaknesses and how best to support each other.

We were married on 6th April 1991, on a beautiful sunny morning. There were 200 guests filling Rhema Chapel, and praying with us as we made our vows to each other and to God. A friend sang a song he had written specially for us, and there was a great deal of love and laughter as well as thankfulness that God had given us to each other. Tara looked wonderful in a dress of cream lace and satin, with her long blonde curls swept over one shoulder and flowers in her hair.

After our reception we had planned to go home for the night before leaving for our honeymoon, but our friends got wind of this and clubbed together to book us a room, dinner and breakfast at the Holiday Inn in Sandton – a real treat. The next day we left for Cathedral Peak in the Drakensberg Mountains, where the views were breathtaking and the mountains behind the hotel looked like velvet. While we were there, I found out where the hotel workers stayed, and went down to their accommodation to share the gospel with them. After five days we moved on to Durban, and then to Shelly Beach to enjoy the sun, sea, and excellent company!

We returned to Johannesburg refreshed and happy, and ready to start our lives together as man and wife in a three-person relationship: a new family with God at the head.

Reaching the family

For some time after our marriage we found visiting my family something of a trial. There was always a certain amount of tension, with sarcastic remarks from my father about people who thought they were "born again" – even though that wasn't term I liked to use. There would be verbal sniping from Andy, too, who always had something derogatory to say about Christianity, though I knew he was just trying to get a reaction out of me. One day he said something sneering about our churchgoing and stuck his hand in my face in a really aggressive manner, but I managed to keep my temper. In the old days I would have flattened him, but I knew I had to turn the other cheek. In any case, I could have knocked him out with a single punch, and I knew that wasn't going to solve anything. I told him, "You can say whatever you want to me. You're my brother and I'll still love you." Tara got tired of the fact that there was some sort of row at every family event we attended.

After a while they stopped criticising us so much. Within six months of our wedding, both Andy and my sister Janice found their own marriages were in trouble. Janice came to visit me one afternoon, driving up in her posh BMW to our tiny cottage. She knew that the whole family was concerned about her because the Roman Catholic Church definitely did not approve of divorce.

I said, "No matter what has happened, I don't condemn you – and I don't believe God condemns you, either." She burst into tears, and I was able to pray with her about her life and her relationship with Jesus.

My grandmother Biddy had always shared the family's attitude to my faith. She was extremely deaf, but strangely, whenever I was talking about Jesus she seemed to be able to hear everything I said. She would turn to me and say stiffly, "We don't need you to tell us about religion, John." One day I was driving past her house and had the same feeling I had had with my mother – I knew God wanted me to call in and speak to her.

"You need to meet God before you die," I told her. "You need to get your life right with him."

This time she was willing to listen, and to think about what I was saying.

"But what if I haven't lived my life that way?" she asked me.

"You've lived it as best you could," I answered. "You did what you thought was right. You can't change the past, but you can change your relationship with God."

Biddy bent her head and prayed with me as I led her in the sinner's prayer, asking Jesus to forgive her and to be her saviour. Then, to my surprise, she went on,

"Lord Jesus, I ask a blessing on John's life and his devotion to you. Keep him and Tara safe as they do your will. Amen."

I was so touched by her love and care for me. She died shortly afterwards, but we had already said our goodbyes, and I was thankful that I had taken that God-given opportunity to bring her to Jesus.

It was a great encouragement to have Biddy and my mother on my side – they were both lovely women who loved God and responded to his call on their lives. My relationship with Janice has always been good, too, and after her divorce she became quietly supportive of me. Andy, on the other hand, is aloof with everyone – not just with me – and my father is still very protective of him, no matter what he does. "He's doing OK," he always says. "Don't you worry about Andy."

My other sister, Carol, never seemed to take much notice of my new-found faith, in spite of the personal attacks Andy used to launch at me every time we met. Carol was usually the most outspoken of us all – always telling everyone what they should be doing. Then she surprised us by announcing that she, too, had become a Christian. She had attended an Alpha course, designed to explain the claims of Jesus to people who have never made a personal commitment to him. She found a new way of understanding her faith, and told me that God was helping her to make sense of her family life.

It was clear to me that I had to rectify my relationship with my father. He had always been a dominant figure in my life, and like most South African boys who grew up under the heavy discipline of a stern father, I nursed a great deal of resentment towards him. I had always been the black sheep of the family, mostly because I was always in trouble, and not behaving as a "religious" family would like. Now I was still playing the same role, but this time my father was angry with me because I was *too* religious! I couldn't win. I had got to the point where there seemed to be little purpose in communicating with him, and I was happy just to stay out of his way, but God wasn't standing for that. He wanted to heal this relationship, too, and I had to make the first move.

One day when I was at my parents' house I began talking about the Lord, and my father got up.

"I'm going out," he said. "I don't need to listen to all this again."

I suddenly felt that I had to try to reach him, and that the best way to do that was to defer to him. I got up, too.

"No, Dad, this is your house. I'll go."

He walked with me to the gate. "Dad," I said, "whatever you say, I'll love you for the rest of my life. But before I go, I just want to hug you."

I put my arms round him and for a moment he resisted me – his body felt rigid and unyielding. Then it was as if something broke inside him, and I felt his arms go round me as he hugged me fiercely to him. I believe that you can release the love of God by the simple act of touching someone, and at that moment the Spirit of God was able to reach his heart as never before. My family had never expressed affection in that way – we never used to hug or kiss each other goodbye – but since then my dad always gives me a hug when we part. I've even added a further challenge, and kiss his cheek, too!

Nothing happened overnight to change my dad, but our relationship is definitely healing. He is still the typical, old-fashioned, dominant South African man, head of his family and brooking no contradiction. But at least we now tolerate each other; we can talk without fighting and agree to disagree. I have discovered that he now prays with my mother every day, and when a friend of his was widowed, this "man's man" ministered to him with great love and gentleness.

Relationships within my family have never been easy, but I believe I have been God's catalyst among them. There is always one person that God grabs hold of, and uses to revolutionise a whole family, and in our case it was me. Since I spoke out about my love for Jesus, our lives have changed. We are all much closer, and more willing to express our love for each other and to reach out to other friends, so the channels for God's transforming love can spread into wider and wider networks.

I have seen the miraculous power of the Holy Spirit transforming me. It's hard to change the instincts taught and reinforced by training and on the battlefield – but God can. He taught me to control the impulse to anger, and the quick recourse to physical violence that had been instilled by the army.

It's hard to touch attitudes that have been part of you since childhood – but God can. He wiped out the racism inscribed in me by my upbringing. The moment when I cradled that old black man in my arms in the hospital ward was a complete revelation to me, for I found Jesus' compassion in my heart, and a new love for my fellow men.

Perhaps it's hardest of all to overcome the resentments and responses of family life, programmed into our family dynamics and part of us since infancy – but God can. He healed the relationships that were closest to me. Now I have a new confidence and freedom in my relationships with every member of my family, because I know that Jesus holds us all in his hand.

CHAPTER (13)

"Crusading" in Africa

AFTER GRADUATING FROM Rhema Bible Training College I knew I wanted to be active for God on the mission field, so Tara and I applied to join Jesus Alive Ministries, which was started by Peter and Anne Pretorius in 1982. Peter had come to the Bible school to share his vision for this mission, which combined relief work with mass open-air gospel crusades in Mozambique and Angola. I was deeply moved when I heard him speak about the work in sub-Saharan Africa, because I was convinced that this was the way we should show the love of Jesus in action – not just by preaching the gospel but by living it, feeding the hungry, healing the sick, and bringing hope to people in need.

I was interviewed and accepted as a trainee Crusade Manager, working under a Portuguese-speaking Crusade Director. Tara and I spent three weeks at the base doing orientation, getting to know the people involved in the Mission as well as its aims and methods. I could see that my military experience in the bush was going to be useful; a great deal of the work was practical, setting up the logistics for oper-ating sites far away in distant parts of the country, but reporting back to central headquarters. We moved out of our cottage, sold most of our furniture, stored our remaining possessions in my van, and set off to do what we most longed to do: work for God full-time in Africa.

Mozambique

Our first assignment was to a crusade in Beira, in Mozambique, which was to be combined with a conference for Christian pastors in the area. When I was a boy I had stood on the border between Rhodesia (now Zimbabwe) and Mozambique, and looked down towards what we knew as the "Beira Corridor". Now, many years later, in a time of peace, I was crossing the border en route to the seaside town of Beira, preparing to share the word of God with people who had once been our enemies.

The border was guarded by soldiers and customs officers, some of whom were looking for bribes, and children clustered round the van, begging for money. In South Africa we were used to computerised customs processing, but in Mozambique we were back to the paper-and-rubber-stamp system. Eventually we cleared our vehicle through passport control and drove off into what was one of the poorest countries in the world. The roads were terrible, full of potholes and littered with abandoned broken-down vehicles, and we drove carefully, taking in the scenery. The vegetation was lush and grew close up to the edge of the road – the climate of Mozambique is semi-tropical – and we passed the remains of fine old brick Portuguese buildings as well as the round African houses built of mud.

The biggest challenge for a white South African was the sense of being white in a black country – it gave us an unfamiliar sense of helplessness. To the rest of the world, of course, it might seem that this was how we had always lived, as a white minority, but that wasn't how it felt under apartheid. Whites made up around ten per cent of the population, yet we owned 80 per cent of the land; the blacks were officially allocated the remaining 20 per cent. As a result, South Africa felt like "our" country. I had been out of the country before, but it was Tara's first visit, and she remarked on the impact this had on her: she said she realised for the first time that Africa was black.

We were towing a caravan, and when we arrived our first job was to attach a tent to it, which was to be our home for the next two months. Most of our work initially was practical: I helped to erect the vast 5,000-seat marquee which JAM was donating to the church in Mozambique, and used my plumbing skills to run a water supply to the facilities. Not everything went smoothly. We set up stage lights and a loud-speaker system, only to find that the generators were not working; then we discovered that a drainage ditch around the tent had not been dug deep enough, and the first rainfall flooded the marquee. These problems increased the pressures on the JAM team, and tested our ability to remain united in the face of difficulty.

Tara, meanwhile, was doing a lot of the office work and typing, as well as running our home, washing all our clothes by hand and boiling all our drinking water for safety. We made many trips to the airport, as the JAM plane brought in pastors from all over Mozambique; I was put in charge of catering and ensured that the field kitchen could provide three meals a day for hundreds of church leaders.

After the pastors' conference we prepared for the main crusade: we put up posters and drove around distributing handbills to publicise the events. We ran a two-week counsellors' course, training local church members to work with us at the crusade, teaching the word of God in English, which was then interpreted into Portuguese and the local African dialect. It was a huge undertaking. Tara ministered at the intercessors' seminar, as we knew that such a work required the prayers of God's people to uphold us and strengthen us.

On our day off, we went to visit the JAM soup kitchen, which had been set up at a medical clinic in nearby Dondo. I was utterly unprepared for what we saw there. The wards were full of victims of the civil war which was still raging in some areas, but there were also many people who were suffering from starvation. One picture will stay with me for ever: a mother sitting helplessly beside a bed where her son lay dying. He looked at first sight about five, but I realised that he didn't have the proportions of a five-year-old: his stick-like arms and legs were too long. He was actually about twelve. His stomach was swollen, not with food but with starvation; his hair had faded from black to a pale ginger colour, and his eyes were glassy. I had seen pictures of famine victims in the past, but now I was seeing it in the flesh, and I was overwhelmed with compassion. I prayed that we might do something to help all the people who became helpless victims of war like this.

The crusade itself was a wonderful experience. Thousands of people gathered to hear the gospel, and many of them came forward to receive prayer and counselling from our teams of dedicated workers. Many of them had been followers of tribal religions, and they cut off their wrist-band fetishes and threw them away as they submitted to the power of the one God, and committed their lives to the love of Jesus.

Life for Angola

After the experience of that first crusade, Tara and I had a better idea what to expect, and our next challenge was an answer to my prayers. As a member of the Rhema Prayer Group I had been praying for peace in Angola, that war-torn country where I had fought ten years before. Now a general ceasefire had been established between the MPLA government and UNITA forces, and JAM had been invited to run city-wide crusades in the west of the country. Once again we spent some time at our headquarters, preparing for a three-month stay, then drove into Namibia (the old South West Africa). We spent one night in Keetmanshoop, staying with a lovely Christian couple who saw the JAM logo on the van and invited us to join them for a barbecue. They already had a team from Youth With A Mission staying with them – they were from Cape Town and were doing outreach in the area, so we shared a happy time of fellowship together.

The next day we drove through the capital,

Windhoek, and on to Oshakati and Ondangwa. I was
excited to see the Air Force Base where we had been
deployed as Fire Force; it was extraordinary to see it
now with its gates unguarded and the military buildings gone. Our old enemy SWAPO was now in power
and a new government installed. It made me reflect
yet again on the futility of war: what had all that
death achieved? So many young men of my generation were still suffering the after-effects of those
traumatic times, and I didn't doubt the same was
true on their side of the conflict. Many of my old
SADF comrades had gone on to fight as mercenaries
in other wars in Africa, and they had given my name
to the paymasters who came looking for soldiers to
bolster their causes. I had been approached several
times and offered money to fight, and I thanked God
that I had put that side of my life behind me. I never
wanted to be in that situation again, where I had to
kill someone just to stay alive myself.

When we crossed into Angola I stopped to talk to
the soldiers guarding the border post; some of them
wore medals they had won when fighting in the conflict which we called Operation Protea. The protea is
the South African national flower; their own name
for the war was probably equally patriotic, but with
my limited Portuguese I couldn't understand it.
Some of my colleagues in the van were nervous about
me engaging in conversation about the war with old
enemies, and admitting that I had fought against
them, but they didn't understand. There's a kind of
comradeship between the survivors of these wars,
even if you have been on opposite sides, a kind of

mutual respect, and a common experience that other people can't share.

Driving through Ondjiva and Xangongo brought back floods of memories. I played back battle scenarios in my mind and thought, "What if", but I knew that was pointless. I had survived, and God had a plan for my life, and I thanked him for it. Now I was going back to pay a kind of debt. I was going to give life where once I took it; and I was bringing the best gift that anyone could bring: the offer of eternal life in Jesus Christ.

Our journey to Lobito took us six days, and was extremely difficult. We encountered roadblocks and lots of soldiers hanging around by the roads with no apparent security purpose, which made us nervous. I was a little apprehensive about being in these situations as a civilian, and I entrusted our mission to God. I was glad that our wives were not with us on the road; they were being flown in by the JAM plane. Fortunately there seemed to be a missionary network of families who were prepared to host us as we travelled. We spent one night at Lubango Air Base as guests of the Missionary Aviation Fellowship.

Our equipment had been shipped from Cape Town to Luanda in two six-metre-long containers, and our Director made the 500-kilometre journey through bandit country to bring the containers to Lobito. We upheld him in prayer and were glad to see him arrive safely. We divided our time between two cities: Lobito and Benguela, about 30 kilometres apart. This meant that we spent a lot of time driving between the two, and we realised that the country was still far from safe. One night we heard automatic rifle fire, and saw people running for cover. When I went out to investigate I found a man continuously firing blanks: he said he was a security guard employed by the city council to keep vagrants out of the stadium where we were based. The following night, however, there were bandits shooting – live ammunition this time – and running riot, and no police in evidence anywhere to restore order.

The crusades were a great success. Once again we publicised them with handbills, getting mobbed by excited children in the villages, and attracting thousands to hear our message. It was wonderful to see people flocking to hear God's message of love, and to realise that we were bringing his word to people who longed for the freedom that is in Christ. It was a privilege for me to minister in Angola, because I knew at first hand what damage had been done in that country by years of war since the Portuguese government left in the mid-1970s. Even when some kind of peace is restored, thousands are still maimed by the millions of landmines which remain concealed in the ground. Every time I preached, I asked forgiveness for the years of apartheid and the South African part in the Angolan conflict, which our government undertook to protect its own regime. I saw people weeping when, as a white man, I repented for the atrocities caused by my own people.

Zambia and Botswana

After these experiences we found great joy in our work with JAM, because we had seen what a difference

Jesus was making in people's lives. I did my first solo crusade in a copper-belt city called Kitwe, in Zambia. We stayed at the Assemblies of God Bible School in our caravan trailer, and met many faithful missionary families who had dedicated their lives to the work of God. Several of these young couples had children, and we watched them and learned from their example of Christian parenting, and began to think ahead to the day when we might have a family of our own.

We had a new team at this mission, and we were blessed by a great outpouring of God's power on us; we saw a unity of love and purpose among our team that we had never witnessed before. We also saw great things happening among the people who came to hear the message: one young woman had carried her disabled sister on her back to attend the Kitwe crusade. We prayed for her healing, and she was able to walk home unaided. Some time later, on our way to a crusade at Chingola, we visited their home and found that her condition had continued to improve, and she was still walking and praising God. Seeing the healing love of Jesus in action like this was a tremendous witness to the people all around, and many of them came to faith through such miracles.

We were not without challenges: on our way to a crusade at Maputo in Mozambique we were warned by the border police that a convoy of trucks just ahead of us had been set alight by bandits, and all the occupants killed. We decided to continue, as we walk by faith and we believed that we were doing God's will in travelling to reach the people of Maputo. All the same, I couldn't help thinking like a soldier. As we approached the scene of the attack, we saw that the Security Forces were also arriving. I turned to Tara and told her, "If there's gunfire, I want you to get out as soon as the van stops, and run diagonally into the bush, on the side away from the attack. I'll join up with you as soon as I've assessed the situation." Thank God we passed through the incident unharmed, and completed our journey in safety.

We had several alarmingly close shaves, with thefts from our van and threats from soldiers and customs officials wanting bribes. In Lusaka I took some money out of the bank and was almost mugged – fortunately I had not lost my soldier's quick reflexes and managed to dodge my assailants. Unfortunately I had not entirely lost my soldier's aggression, and I'm ashamed to say that I pursued them up the road, ready to hit them with a piece of pipe I had in the car. Then I realised that passers-by were being treated to the spectacle of a missionary with the JAM logo on his van chasing the muggers down the road and shouting threats. I returned to the van, where Tara was shaking her head at me. I realised that God was still working on me – and there was still a lot to do.

In spite of these events, we found Zambia a warm and friendly place. The people were easy to love and had tremendous joy in their hearts. The President had publicly committed the nation to God at his inauguration, and it was almost fashionable to be a Christian. I became friendly with the Commanding Officer of the regional police force, who was a believer, and he gave us permission for a city-wide Jesus March. President Chiluba himself invited the entire crusade team for tea, and we were delighted that God's missionaries could be shown such public approval. He received us at his stately home, a small man sitting in a huge chair covered with leopard skin. He poured us tea from a silver teapot, and I said, "We should be serving you, sir, as President."

"No," he replied, "it is an honour to serve the ministers of God."

We returned to South Africa, where I left Tara while I made a short trip to deliver a generator in Zambia. While there I felt ill and was treated for tick-bite fever, but when the symptoms did not improve I saw another doctor, who diagnosed malaria and gave me the right medication. Then I had a call from the JAM General Manager, telling me that Tara was ill, too, and had been rushed to hospital. This was even more worrying, because by now we knew that she was expecting our first baby. I returned to find her recovered, but we faced astronomical medical bills for her stay in hospital.

One more mission, in Botswana, was an eye-opener for me. When I visited the capital, Gaborone, I saw many mixed couples – one partner white, the other black. This had been forbidden in South Africa until 1991, when the last of the old apartheid laws were repealed, so it wasn't something we were used to seeing. Couples who wanted to marry had been forced to leave South Africa, and many of them had settled here. There were other South Africans here, too: political refugees who were not considered to be South African citizens because they were not allowed to obtain passports. Once again I felt a kind of guilt on behalf of my country and my government, who had encouraged such destructive prejudice.

I was delighted to find that the church leaders in Botswana had no prejudice against white South Africans who had come to share the good news of Jesus. We had several days of wonderful crusading and ministered the word of God to hundreds of young people. Botswana seemed to be an affluent country – one of the few self-sufficient countries in Africa. We had a well-attended business breakfast in a top hotel, where we were able to speak to a large group of men and women who would never have come to join us at our dusty crusade site. We also had an inspiring believers' meeting in the city, where people from all the churches came together, and many were filled with the Holy Spirit. They were empowered to go on witnessing to their friends and neighbours in Botswana, after our mission had moved on.

CHAPTER 14

A Gift from God

BACK IN JOHANNESBURG we began preparing for our next round of crusades, planned for Zaire (now called the Democratic Republic of Congo). Sadly, after we left Angola the peace accord broke down, and civil war flared up again. In the subsequent riots all our equipment, which we had left stored in containers, was destroyed. We needed to replace everything if we were to keep our promise to the churches in Zaire.

Everyone worked furiously to meet the deadline, and with generous help from our international supporters we managed to purchase everything we needed – tent, lighting poles, stage and sound system. The printing department was producing all the posters, handbills and the all-important follow-up booklets, which gave us a record of people who had expressed an interest in knowing more, and gave the enquirer a printed summary of the gospel. After work everyone went down to the function hall, where we set up a production line for folding and collating the bundles of papers and placing them into boxes ready for transport.

Our other crusade manager had already left for Lubumbashi, in the south of Zaire. He planned to drive up to the diamond-mine area where we were holding the crusade, but found that the roads were impassable in a conventional car, so he arranged to take a plane to Mbuji-Mayi, in central Zaire. Someone had to travel up to deliver the extra $1,500 in cash to pay the pilot, and I was asked to do the job. The journey would have a double purpose: I could also do a trial run on the roads from Johannesburg to Mbuji-Mayi, to check out the route for the huge 35-tonne crusade rig which had to make the trip in time for our launch.

We would be travelling in a brand new four-wheel-drive pickup, with large wheels for extra ground clearance, but when I studied the map I realised that for at least a thousand kilometres there were no proper roads. It was still the rainy season and we would inevitably get bogged down in the mud, so we equipped ourselves with picks and shovels to dig ourselves out when necessary. We added extra water and diesel containers, plenty of food supplies, and all the finished printed materials, and set off northwards into Central Africa.

The hardest part for me was that Tara was staying at home: she was six months pregnant with our first child, and couldn't travel with us. I was going to be away for three months.

We drove north-east across South Africa and crossed the great River Limpopo into Zimbabwe. Then we drove right across the country to the border with Zambia, where we arranged a three-day transit permit, and headed for the capital, Lusaka. There we went to the Zairean embassy to request visas to enter the restricted diamond-mining area. This took three days, and it was while we were waiting that we realised that, back in our own country, history was unfolding. It was April 1994, and the first democratic elections were being held in South Africa. The black workers who were with us were shaking their heads in disbelief. For the first time ever, black people were allowed to vote alongside the whites for the government of their choice.

It was several days before we heard the result: the African National Congress had won 60 per cent of the vote; the National Party came second with 20 per cent, and the Inkatha Freedom Party came third, with ten per cent. In May, Nelson Mandela was inaugurated as President of South Africa, and Thabo Mbeki as his First Deputy. With great tact and diplomacy he appointed the National Party leader, F W de Klerk, as his Second Deputy, and named the Zulu Chief Buthelezi as Home Affairs Minister, thus including the opposition parties in the cabinet. Far away in Zambia we celebrated this breakthrough in South African politics; we hoped that the new government would find a peaceful way forward, and try to heal some of the savage wounds which apartheid had caused in our society.

Armed with our visas, we crossed the border into Zaire and tackled the customs department. We knew that corruption was rife among the border guards, and we weren't surprised to find that we had to buy new vehicle registration papers, even though the ones we had were in order. I dug my heels in, though, when a military officer said, "You have to pay £20 for road protection."

"I've got all the protection I need," I said, and left the building. Outside, I found that the truck was surrounded by several paratroopers armed with AK 47s. I took one look at them and said, "I'll be right back!" and went back and paid up. It was the sensible solution.

Arriving in Lubumbashi, we paid the pilot who had airlifted our other manager to Mjubi-Mayi, and picked up the chairman of the crusade committee, Yemme Tumbalupa, who would be our guide on the road to Kananga. It was a terrifying journey; soon the tarmac gave out and we were travelling on unmetalled roads. In some places the ground had almost dried out, but in others we had to negotiate our way through standing pools of water and thick mud. We drove from dawn to dusk each day, sleeping and eating beside the vehicle at the roadside, and the further north we went, the denser the bush became, slowing our progress even more. We crossed and re-crossed the Zaire River on flimsy-looking bridges – I wondered how the huge crusade rig would manage on those.

One afternoon there was a torrential downpour, and we approached a dip in the road which was completely flooded. I could see the road coming up again on the far side of the water, but I had no idea how deep it would be in the middle. We had to get across, so I prayed to God to keep us safe, engaged the four-wheel drive in first gear and revved the motor. As we set off the front wheels suddenly dropped and water flooded over the bonnet – I had to use the windscreen wipers to see where we were going. By the grace of God we reached the other side safely, and only then did I turn round to see the terrified faces of my passengers.

We went on like this for days on end: I was the

only qualified driver, so I had to keep going, no matter how exhausted I was. I was grateful for my military training and the *vasbyt* that taught me to dig deep into myself for reserves of determination. When we finally arrived in Kananga we had been travelling for fourteen days; remarkably, we had had only two punctures.

We started to set up our headquarters in Kananga; I must admit that I was already tired and dispirited, and I was missing Tara badly. We had promised to keep in close touch, but there was no post or telephone system, so I recorded audiocassettes to send off with the JAM plane when it came for the crusade. At the same time, it was interesting to be in such a different part of Africa, and to be so closely accepted into the local society. The crusade chairman's uncle was in trouble – he had broken his code of honour as a shepherd by selling two of the family's sheep – and we had the privilege of being allowed to attend the tribal hearing. We drove to one of the many small villages nearby, stopping off at the police station to collect a local gendarme.

The village elders were seated at a table under the shade of a huge tree in the centre of the village, and the chairman and I were asked to join them. The villagers sat and listened to the evidence, and the chief cross-questioned the man. Then the elders debated among themselves and came to the conclusion that he was guilty. The gendarme came and bound the prisoner's hands with rope, and we were asked to transport him to the local prison, where he would be sentenced by a local magistrate. I was fascinated to see the way the cultures worked together for local justice, and I felt it was an honour to be allowed to take part in the process.

I was called from Kananga to Mbuji-Mayi to help set up the site for our first crusade, as once again we were behind schedule. The rig trailer had overturned on the road, and we lost several days in unpacking the cargo, digging a trench alongside the vehicle, and righting it with the help of a block and tackle. I helped the rigging crew, working day and night erecting the stage, lights, and ten massive 100-kilogramme speakers. When the crusade started I realised why we needed such a huge public address system: I had never seen so many people in one place. Over 300,000 people gathered each night to hear our evangelist, Peter Pretorius, preach the word of God, and thousands came forward for prayer and to give their names to the teams of counsellors waiting for them. In the following weeks every one of these would be followed up by the local churches, offered friendship, teaching and prayer, and encouraged to accept Jesus into their lives. I was overcome with joy when I saw how glad they were to hear God's word.

After the Mbuji-Mayi crusade we dismantled the rig and rebuilt it in Kananga two weeks later. During the time of preparation I had realised how ill-prepared I was to minister to these people: the crusade chairman was the only person in Kananga who spoke English, and he had to interpret for me wherever I went. Zaire had been a Belgian colony and many people spoke French as well as their African languages, but my French was appalling! Nevertheless I was invited to preach at most of the churches participating in the crusade, and God placed a message in my heart which I shared wherever I went. It was that the power of the Holy Spirit was freely available to every one of us; we have only to ask and open our hearts to receive him. I could say this out of my own experience; there had been many times when I knew I was not acting from my own strength or wisdom, but God gave me the power to work for him. I prayed for many of the believers, and they were filled with the Spirit. People wept as they confessed their sins and laid their hearts before Jesus, and many were healed in his name.

I was excited to see so many thousands of decisions to follow Christ, but by the end of the crusade I was feeling ill and tired. I was sick and unable to eat, and kept losing track of time, so that I wasn't sure whether I had remembered to take my anti-malaria drugs. After a while I began to feel the characteristic fevers and chills, and knew that I was suffering from malaria again, but we were scheduled to stay on for another month. There was all the follow-up work and liaison with the churches to get started, as well as packing up the crusade rig for the long journey home. I was feeling worse and worse, but out here in this poverty-stricken country I knew there was no suitable medical support to help me.

One day I had to take our crusade chairman's mother to the airport at Kananga, and after I had dropped her off I sat for a while in the car, shaking with fever, and trying to gather the energy for the drive back into town. Just then I saw one of the airport officials waving at me and speaking in a jumble of French which I couldn't understand. Eventually we found someone to interpret, and he said,

"We've had a radio message from the JAM headquarters in South Africa. Your wife has gone into labour three weeks early. You need to set off at once."

It was a miracle that I was at the airport that day to receive the message; I don't know how long it would have been before someone managed to contact us. I was feeling terrible, but I knew I had to make that journey, and once again I was the only driver available. I sped back and collected my belongings, and set out at 3 a.m. to drive half the length of Africa.

As I set off I said, "Lord, I need to spend some time in prayer before you for this journey."

God spoke to my heart: "Don't worry about that. I've got people praying. All you need to do is drive!"

We seemed to fly over the roads. I knew that our intercessors were praying for me as I drove, and every roadblock was miraculously unmanned until we reached Kamina, 650 kilometres to the south. There an official confiscated our spare diesel supply, and we drove on until we ran out of fuel just outside Lubumbashi, at the border. It was the early hours of the morning, and we thought there was no way we would find any help, but we saw a single dim light bouncing towards us along the empty road. To our joy it turned out to be a truck with a friendly driver, who siphoned some diesel from his tank into ours so that we could make it into town. We had travelled day and night for three days, stopping only to refuel and eat one hot meal by the roadside, and we were all exhausted.

We managed to buy some more fuel and carried on to the border with Zambia. There we met up with another JAM worker who had news. "Brother, you have baby girl," he said in his sweet broken English. "Wife is fine." I threw my hands in the air and shouted "Hallelujah!" I had known in my heart that God was taking care of Tara, but it was so good to hear the words.

In Zambia we stopped at the house of a Canadian missionary friend, where I washed for the first time in three days, slept for three hours, and began to feel better. Then I pressed on, driving south to the border with South Africa, where I was held up for a couple of hours and snatched some more sleep while I waited for the border crossing to open for the day.

Back in Johannesburg Tara and our newborn baby were ready to leave hospital, but as she waited to be picked up, Tara was praying, "God, I wish John had been able to come to the hospital for me." She was sitting on her bed, staring out of the window, when I walked into the ward.

I said, "Is that my baby you're holding?" and she turned around in disbelief. I was exhausted, dirty and hungry, but so happy to be there. I had covered half the African continent in five nights and four days.

Jade was our miracle baby. Quite apart from the emergency surrounding her birth, we knew that if that message had not recalled me from the field, I would probably have died – there was no proper malaria treatment available in that part of Zaire. As it was I was able to get treatment and rest at home, and spend time with Tara and the baby. Once again

God had sustained me and held my life safely in his hands. Two weeks later, when we invited our family to Jade's dedication at the church, I promised God that we would trust him with the life of our little family wherever he took us. I didn't realise that the next step I took with him would take me face to face with death yet again.

CHAPTER 15

Death in Rwanda

WHENEVER I WAS TRAVELLING in Africa I tried to keep in touch with the news by listening to the BBC World Service and to Voice of America's "Africa Tonight" programme. In April 1994, while I was still in Kananga, I listened with mounting horror as reports began to come in of events in Kigali, Rwanda. A plane carrying the presidents of Rwanda and Burundi had been shot down, killing both men and many of their staff. No one knew who was responsible, but the presidential guard immediately began a campaign of revenge. Gradually it became clear that something devastating was happening, as a tide of death swept across the country.

The root of the problem was an ancient conflict between two groups, the Hutus and the Tutsis. Until it became independent Rwanda had been governed by Belgium, which favoured the Tutsis, giving them better jobs and educational opportunities. In 1959 the Hutus rebelled and killed thousands of Tutsis, while many more fled to Uganda, Zaire and Tanzania. When the Belgians withdrew in 1962, the Hutus took over the government.

President Habyarimana was a Hutu, and when his plane crashed the ruling officials responded by blaming the Tutsis and encouraging their systematic slaughter. An unofficial militia group called

Interahamwe ("those who attack together") was formed, and they were joined by many ordinary people. In some cases the soldiers forced Hutu civilians to murder their Tutsi neighbours. They also killed other moderate Hutus who were thought to sympathise with the RPF (Rwandan Patriotic Front), formed by Tutsi refugees in Uganda, who had been waging intermittent war on the regime since 1990.

The army, police and *Interahamwe* had guns; the Hutu civilians had clubs and machetes; together they killed thousands in every town and village. Women were raped and then hacked to death; people of all ages were shot or clubbed to death in their homes or in the churches where they had sought shelter. Bodies were left to rot in the streets or were thrown into Lake Kivu. Around 800,000 people were killed in around thirteen weeks – three-quarters of the Tutsi population – and the horror was indescribable. Thousands of Tutsis fled across the border to Tanzania and Zaire, where international agencies established refugee camps to care for them.

The RPF continued its battle against the Hutu regime, and in July it succeeded in capturing Kigali and declared a ceasefire. However, this victory provoked another wave of refugees. As the RPF advanced, over a million Hutus – including many of those involved in the genocide – fled to the camps in Zaire, already filled with displaced Tutsis. The country could not support so many extra people, and they were starving. In a very short space of time, there was a humanitarian crisis of extraordinary proportions.

I wept as I listened to the news reports, and

prayed for the people in the Great Lakes area, caught up in violence and hatred once again. I lifted them up to God and asked that their physical needs might be met, that their emotional scars might be healed, and that their deep spiritual hunger would be filled with the love of Jesus. Even as I prayed, I knew that God would use me somehow: I am a man of prayer, but I'm also a man of action! I knew I wanted to be involved in helping.

Only a few weeks later the JAM General Manager asked me if I would be prepared to get involved with the relief efforts. A shipment of 2,000 tonnes of maize and medical supplies was being transported by truck from sea ports to the refugee camps in Zaire, and they needed someone to lead a team of workers to help with the distribution. I asked Tara if she minded me going, but she simply replied, "You must do what's in your heart." She knew it meant another three-month separation.

Goma refugee camps

Goma is in south-eastern Zaire, on the shores of Lake Kivu. As we landed at the airport after a ten-hour journey, I looked out of the window and saw cattle and goats grazing on the overgrown airfield; young shepherd boys chased their animals off the tarmac as we approached. French and American forces were based in tents beside the runway, and there was clearly a massive military operation going on, with transport planes offloading food and equipment supplies.

We drove through the city to our accommodation, which was a rented house in the university area. On the way we saw long lines of children queuing at tankers to collect purified water: Lake Kivu was polluted by hundreds of dead bodies, and a cholera epidemic was already raging. Some people had been drinking the dirty water from potholes in the road. All the trees along the roadside had been stripped of their branches, and men on motor scooters were ferrying huge loads of firewood out of the city. In the distance I could see a wide expanse of blue plastic, shimmering the sun: it was thousands of makeshift shelters, made of stick frames covered with the blue plastic tarpaulins provided by UNHCR (United Nations High Commission for Refugees): the Mugunga Camp.

Jesus Alive Ministries was not the only organisation arriving to help. There were also international relief teams from the Christian Relief Network, Samaritan's Purse, World Vision, the Red Cross, the World Food Programme, UNICEF (the United Nations Children's Fund), Oxfam and many others. All these groups had to be organised so that we worked together and did not duplicate our effort. The Israeli army had set up a field hospital some distance away in the path of the fleeing refugees, and they were doing a wonderful job in tending the worst of the wounded, and distributing food and water so that people could manage the journey to safety.

Together, the three camps in the area held around a million people. Rows of tents had been arranged into "streets", and pastors had been appointed for each section. There was certainly a need for spiritual support, just as much as for food.

The camps were full of people who had lost everything, and often what they wanted most was someone to talk to. They wanted to tell their story, and pour out all their fear and horror. Families had been separated in their desperate flight, and UNICEF was taking photographs of the children in the orphanages and posting them on noticeboards in the camps, in an effort to reunite them with their parents.

Some of the people we were helping were themselves killers – in among the refugees were members of *Interahamwe*, and they were vicious fighters. They would still kill a Tutsi if they saw one, and they expressed no remorse for the massacres they had incited. Sometimes I would look into the eyes of a man and see only murder, and the soldier in me wanted to take him on. I pushed the instinct down, because I knew that violence only breeds violence. I was here to bring peace, not to fight.

My job was to lead a team which went into the camp each day. I was working with the World Food Programme which was co-ordinating food collection and distribution – they had trucks running continuously, bringing in food and treated water. I would meet the twelve-metre trucks at the border crossing, check them and escort them back to the camp. We were equipped with two-way radios because it was a dangerous run: several convoys had been attacked and robbed. Then we would take the vehicles to the distribution points and unload the 50-kilogramme sacks of grain. We had to have extra security to keep back the excited crowds when the food arrived; the pastors oversaw the distribution to ensure that the elderly and the children received their weekly ration of the precious cooking oil and maize to make into porridge.

As we drove down the bumpy roads towards the camp, we had to be alert to avoid children running along behind the trucks, ready to pick up any stray kernels spilling from the sacks. They were from families who refused to come and live in the camps, and most of them were starving. Every morning we would see grass mats rolled up beside the road, covering the bodies of those who had died during the night. Special vehicles had to be dispatched, their drivers wearing white overalls, with masks to protect them from the stench of death. They collected the bodies and buried them in mass graves, covered with lime.

Our three nurses were kept busy inoculating people and treating their illnesses – dysentery, yellow fever, cholera and malaria. We did everything we could to prevent the spread of disease. New arrivals at the orphanage were bathed (the children screaming at their first experience of a soapy sponge) and given new clothes, donated by charities. Their old clothes were burned. Some of these children were so traumatised that they couldn't even cry: they would stand and stare blankly at you. Often it took months of patient care just to get a child to smile. I used to organise games and play football with them, but there just weren't enough hands available to pick up all these children and give them the love they needed.

Some of them had watched their parents die; others had seen their parents killing their neighbours, and joined in, caught up in the killing frenzy. If you gave them pencils and paper, they drew only pictures of dead bodies and people waving machetes. Death rates among these children were high: they would come into hospital and die overnight, from even the slightest ailments. I know they were weakened by lack of food, but often it seemed that they simply lacked the will to live. We had one little boy who suffered from meningitis and yellow fever, yet he survived everything – he was a tough kid and he wanted to live.

It was exhausting work, both physically and emotionally. At night I was glad to get away from the filth of the camp; I always left my shoes outside the house, and washed from head to foot when I got home. The camp was filled to capacity with hundreds of thousands of people living in impossible conditions. There were always lost children crying; women pounding maize corn into meal or cooking it over open fires; people carrying loads of firewood from the stripped trees outside; men laughing and drinking beer; people talking and shouting; the noise was tremendous. And among them all, you would see the young men in combat uniforms hanging around in groups – the remains of the *Interahamwe*, a reminder that violence was never far away.

In this situation it was easy for people to ask, "Where is God in all this suffering?" My only answer was to turn my eyes to the picture of Jesus on the cross, dying for the sake of others, to know that God was alongside us, sharing in our pain. I took every opportunity to talk to people about Jesus, because I knew from experience that only God's love is strong enough to bring peace into your heart when you have been involved in violence.

One day my interpreter suggested that I might like to meet a small group of Hutu soldiers. They were not living in the camp; expecting a revenge attack from the Tutsis, they were dug in to a defensive position in the bush. When we parked our truck we were led by a tortuous route to their secret encampment. I told them that I, too, had been a soldier and fought in the Angolan war, and I recounted how I had given my life to the Lord and what a difference it had made to me. When I prayed, several of them responded and asked God's forgiveness; afterwards we had a wonderful time of worship together, and they danced and sang for joy, out there in the bush – hidden from other people but close to God.

It was a great source of joy to see how God was working through his people in these awful conditions. Often the humanitarian aid workers would say, "We can help with people's physical needs but we can't heal the emotional damage. Can your church workers help us?" It was the patient love of the Christians of all denominations that was making a real difference in reaching people's hearts. They were generally trusted, and it was wonderful to see how the church had regrouped in the refugee camps, being asked to administer the social infrastructures including health, security and food distribution.

On one occasion I was invited to speak at an ordination service, where over a hundred young men were being anointed for God's service. Thousands of us sat in the hot sun for a five-hour service; FM microphones were used and radios all over the camp were tuned in to share in the event. There was a real hunger for God and I was thankful that I was able to play a part in reaching so many people with his love.

Gitarama

We were expecting an aircraft supply run, and I heard the welcome news that Tara was flying in to see me for three days; she had left Jade with her mum. The flight was coming in to Kigali Airport, so I drove into Rwanda with a young colleague who had just joined JAM. Security was tight at the border, as there had been several *Interahamwe* attacks in recent days; we had to unpack everything while our vehicle was thoroughly checked. There were RPF patrols everywhere, often driving saloon cars they had confiscated, with all the doors and windows removed so the soldiers could deploy quickly in case of trouble. There were crashed and burnt-out trucks littered along the roadsides, and we drove through several deserted villages, eerily silent after the hubbub of the camp.

Kigali Airport was functioning but bore the scars of war: every building was pockmarked with bullet holes, and several bore blast holes from grenades and mortar bombs. It was wonderful to see Tara, and it hurt to realise how much time we were spending apart because of the ministry we were committed to. I knew then that one day we would have to move on from JAM and build a life for our family together.

We collected supplies for the JAM orphanage and drove to Gitarama, 35 kilometres south-west of Kigali. The orphanage was based in a school, next door to the cathedral where the priests and the bishop had been killed. The RPF had found hundreds of bodies piled in a storeroom and left to rot; most of them bore the marks of rifle shots and wounds from spears and even farm implements. Now they had been cleared in a rough and ready way, but I saw a human skull in the garden. In those horrific times there was no opportunity for the reverent disposal of human remains, and the bodies just had to be buried as fast as possible.

Several hundred children attended the school, and we heard some of their stories. One girl told how her family had been cut down in a machete attack on her village. Her mother and father fell on top of her and died; their bodies protected her, and though she was badly injured by the blades and left for dead, she managed to escape. She made her way to her grandparents' village only to find that everyone there was dead, and wandered aimlessly until she was picked up by an *Interahamwe* band who threw her into a river. She was rescued by a French military officer who brought her to the orphanage. When she was asked about her miraculous survival, she said, "When I am older I want to be a missionary and find the people who hurt me, so I can take them the love and forgiveness of Jesus!"

I met the new Governor of Gitarama, an army major who had led several hundred men to defeat the Hutu forces. When he heard that I had been a soldier he told me about the various battles he had fought, and showed me the bullet wounds he had suffered. He was trying to organise a city that had to begin again from scratch, with most of the population dead or departed. What amazed me was the fact that many Tutsi Roman Catholic clergy had come back into the country as soon as possible, determined to help rebuild their communities. I asked one of them how he had the faith to start such a massive undertaking, and he replied, "The Roman Catholic Church has a 500-year vision for the Rwandan nation. We can't let any single uprising affect that."

Everything depended on peace being brokered and sustained, in the face of continuing unrest throughout the country. At the time of the genocide, the rest of the international community was reluctant to get involved. The United Nations had pulled out in late April, after the murder of ten Belgian paratroopers; the USA was recovering from the debacle in Somalia, when many of its troops had been killed, and was unwilling to enter a similar scenario. Only France had run a small operation in south-west Rwanda, saving some victims from the massacre. It made me wonder whether the Western nations really cared about what happened in Africa, and whether the UN peacekeeping forces could do any good at all.

It was easy to be despondent about the state of so many African nations, but as I kissed Tara goodbye and made my way back to Goma, I knew that all I could do was the work that lay before me. Helping, supporting, comforting, and telling people about Jesus, one by one. I couldn't change the world, but God could – one heart at a time. Within two years, JAM would be running crusades in Goma, Bukavu and Bujumbura, Burundi, where thousands of people made decisions to follow Jesus.

CHAPTER (16)

Mission South Africa

IN 1995 I WAS ORDAINED at Rhema Church, as a minister in the International Fellowship of Christian Churches. I was sure that this was an important next step for me, but beyond that I had no idea where God wanted me to be. The following year Tara, Jade and I went on an extended visit to the UK, where I was able to minister in several churches and present a course at a Bible school in the Midlands. We liked England and made some good friends during our stay, and I believed that at some time in the future we might be called to work here, but we both felt that this was not the time. We returned home to South Africa and Jesus Alive Ministries: Tara worked as Production Secretary in the Video Department, and I was appointed as Special Projects Co-ordinator.

There was one difficulty about this new job – I was expected to represent JAM at all sorts of fund-raising and publicity events. I had plenty of experience of public speaking at churches in the run-up to crusades, but I needed a new range of skills for this work, so I was sent on a public relations course at Damelin Business College. I graduated with a first-class diploma and the highest pass mark that year in the entire country – not bad for someone with only a Standard 8 education! As part of our final assessment we had to give a short presentation about a pet subject. The other students talked about everyday things – bus trips or swimming with dolphins – but I spoke about "this man I met". I talked about how special he was and what interesting ideas he had, and explained at the end that the man was Jesus. Some of the audience smiled, and others looked embarrassed. I wasn't sure how the examiners would take it, but to my relief they thought it was great. It was a twelve-minute ministry, and they said they were only deducting marks because I didn't go the whole way and finish with the altar call!

I enjoyed my new job, giving talks at churches, house groups and Bible schools, and doing some fund-raising for the orphanage at Gitarama. In 1997 Tara gave birth to our son, Liam Jordan, and I was proud and happy that this time I was with her and able to see our child born. The doctor joked as he delivered him and said, "Here comes your second daughter."

"I know it's a boy," I replied. "I asked God for a little boy."

Then everyone stopped what they were doing as I took my son in my arms and dedicated him to God – they said afterwards that they had never had a dedication in surgery before.

JAM was developing an Emergency Relief Team, and they asked me to oversee and equip this arm of the ministry. My years in the field had given me plenty of experience in leading and training teams, so in July I took on nine university students who had volunteered for training during their winter vacation. I bought dome tents, water purifiers, bush showers, cookers and everything else necessary for living in the bush for months, organised a four-day orientation and first aid course, and then put the students on a bus to Mozambique. I drove there separately, with one assistant, in a four-wheel-drive vehicle towing a huge trailer.

Initially we stayed at the JAM orphanage and food distribution centre at Pambarra, near the east coast, living in the staff house. The students had various tasks: sorting donated clothes into bundles, helping in the fields, caring for the goats, and digging the well deeper (there was a drought). After a week or so we set out into the bush, marching to our new location, where we pitched our tents, dug latrines and gathered firewood. Nine hundred bundles of clothing and a couple of reinforced 200-litre drums were transported to our new camp, along with food supplies, and word went out to the local inhabitants that a soup kitchen would open the next day.

Early the following morning we lit fires under the drums, and set about cooking the nutritious maize porridge made with added milk powder, oil and soya beans. Hundreds of families arrived, queuing patiently in the hot sun; most of the children showed the tell-tale signs of malnutrition. We served the food and handed out bundles of clothes, and we were humbled to see the delight on people's faces – many of them had been using strips of soft bark as clothing. Several of the students wept openly as they realised for the first time the extent of the poverty in the area, and the opportunity they had been given to show God's love to these people.

The next day we packed up the camp and the students walked back to our base in Pambarra. We had supper with the JAM Project Manager, and afterwards the young people got out their guitars and worshipped God in songs and prayers. As I listened to them I felt the love of God burning strongly in my heart. I went outside to be alone for a while, and said to God, "Lord, I submit my life to you. I will stop trying to please other people, and acting in my own strength. Instead I will learn to rest in you and enjoy your love." Before returning home, we took the students for a few days' relaxation at the beach, but the whole time I felt uplifted by my renewed commitment to the Lord. I knew that he would show me in his good time what he had planned for me.

In this frame of mind, I began to examine our current life in South Africa. I realised that somewhere along the line I had lost some of the enthusiasm that had always fired my ministry. Partly I felt that working for a large missionary organisation was too restrictive – we had shared aims and communal targets, but often I found that I was having to fit into someone else's rigid plan. I was losing my individuality. Additionally, the work was demanding, both physically and spiritually, yet after several years it was also too familiar. I needed a change of pace and a change of focus.

I tried to deal with my dissatisfaction by setting myself new challenges: I ran the Comrades' Marathon, a gruelling 87 kilometres from Pietermaritzburg to Durban. This race was particularly demanding because it was the equivalent of two normal marathons, and if you hadn't managed the first half in under five hours, you were not allowed to continue. It was a great personal achievement to complete it for the second time (I ran my first in 1989, when I was still only 27, and considerably fitter!).

I also did a parachute jump into water with a group of ex-Bats – we jumped from a C130 into the Roodeplaat Dam. It was a fantastic feeling to be airborne once more, and I remembered how much I had loved the team spirit, the anticipation and the exhilaration of the descent. After our landing we all got talking, catching up on old times, and I realised how different my life had become. Some of the guys asked me what line of work I was in now, and were pretty surprised by the answer! It was a great opportunity to share the gospel. Lots of them had continued to fight in various conflicts, and carried on with the wild life that I had once lived. Several of them had married, but most of those had divorced once or even twice; often their families were fragmented and they didn't seem able to sustain relationships in the face of their drinking habits and their tendency to aggression and violence. I could see the route my life could so easily have taken, and I thanked God for Tara and my precious babies, sleeping safely at home. When we reminisced about our wartime experiences, it was like talking about someone else's life.

One day I was chatting to a tough guy I hadn't seen in 16 years, and, as we talked about the war, he grew quieter and paler. Then he got up abruptly from the table and went to the bathroom – it was clear he was having a panic attack. After a minute or two I followed him and asked him through the door, "Do you mind if I pray for you?"

"Do it," he said. There was a pause, and then he said in a small voice, "Johnny, can you pray that the dreams go away?"

I remembered the horror nightmares I used to have, and realised what a work Jesus had done in my heart and my mind, making even my subconscious safe from those terrifying memories.

I knew that I still had a mission to preach the gospel, but I also knew that I would have no peace until I followed God's leading – I had to trust him and move out into work without the support of a big missionary organisation behind me. I went back to Sean's first teaching: "Do whatever your hand finds to do, for God is with you" (1 Samuel 10:7). In JAM I had been travelling around Africa, to Mozambique, Angola, Zambia, Botswana, Zaire and Rwanda. Now I wanted to serve God in my own country, South Africa, as it worked out its new identity.

Since the end of apartheid, many aspects of life have changed. We have a true democracy and majority government; South Africa calls itself the "Rainbow Nation" where all races live together. We have eleven official languages, and probably the most complicated National Anthem in the world, which begins with the Nguni and Sotho versions of *Nkosi sikeleli Afrika* (God bless Africa), continues with four lines of the Afrikaans *Die stem van Suid-Afrika* (The call of South Africa) and finishes with four lines in English.

These things are all symbols of a commitment to unity and equality, but in reality there is still a great deal to do before the damage done by apartheid is healed. For many whites in South Africa, change has happened too fast, and they are still trying to come to terms with the end of segregation, but for the blacks it has been too slow. Too many people are still waiting and hoping for better living standards, housing, education and opportunities – all things I took for granted when I was growing up as a white South African. In 1995, in an inspired move, Archbishop Desmond Tutu set up the Truth and Reconciliation Commission, to investigate apartheid-era human-rights abuses, but there is still resentment and anger in many hearts. Only Jesus can bring peace and love into those hidden places where people still suffer, and I wanted to spread that message of God's love.

In the autumn of 1997 I was released from JAM with the blessing of the evangelist, Peter Pretorius, and given a VW van, a trailer and a generator to help me in my new ministry. We registered a new organisation, Surrender to the Cross Ministries, with its own board of directors to oversee the work, and moved into an apartment in Johannesburg, though Tara continued to work at JAM. I had a vision to run crusades in South Africa and to take the gospel to prisons, schools and business fellowships, and I gathered a small team to help me.

I ran my first crusade at Zandspruit squatter camp, north-west of Johannesburg. Once the Pass Laws and Groups Areas Acts had been repealed, blacks were free to live and work where they liked, but of course they seldom had the means to buy homes. They no longer had to live in the black townships, but instead these squatter camps of shanty homes grew up around the expensive white suburbs, as blacks tried to live closer to their place of work. Thousands of families lived there, sharing water and toilets in communal blocks, and building flimsy homes of wood and metal.

It was a wonderful feeling to bring the crusade atmosphere home to South Africa. The local church band praised and worshipped God with great joy, and the church youth group did the Harlem Shuffle to the music, which drew a crowd of curious onlookers. More than 70 people prayed to receive Jesus as their Lord and Saviour, many were baptised in the Holy Spirit, and some were healed.

The next crusade was at Estcourt near Durban, and again we witnessed the power of God to change lives. In the past the churches were segregated, and white churches had nothing to do with their black neighbours, even if the churches were the same denomination. Now, for the first time in the history of the country, the churches were working together, and this in itself was a great witness to the liberating love of God. Over a hundred adults and a couple of hundred children responded to the message of faith, and they were all linked up to the seven local churches and the discipleship training school.

After this I was invited to Venda, in the Northwest Province near the Zimbabwe border. On the Sunday morning I shared my testimony in a radio interview, and in the afternoon I preached in a church – as usual in Africa, the service lasted for five hours. On Monday we were allowed into the local prison. There were 47 prisoners in the maximum-security wing, and 35 of them gave their hearts to the Lord; we then preached to 300 short-term prisoners. One of the officers commented that he had never heard the gospel preached like that, with a message of personal salvation: he didn't seem surprised that so many had responded. As the prison didn't have a swimming pool, we brought in a portable pool and filled it using a fire hydrant. Around 70 prisoners were baptised.

Back in Johannesburg we were still finding new areas of ministry in conjunction with Jacques Scharnik. At Christmas we went out with gifts of roses and chocolates, and gave them to the prostitutes who worked the streets over the holidays. The girls would ask, "What do you want?" and were amazed when we told them we had free gifts for them, because Jesus had freely given his life for them.

In 1998 an organisation called Word of Life Ministries ran a week-long crusade called *Jabulani* (Rejoice) in Joubert Park, Johannesburg. We were helping the evangelist, Ed Elliott, to follow up the people who had expressed an interest in knowing more about Jesus Christ, but we didn't have a church to invite them to. We needed premises, and so we rented a large room in Highpoint Building in Hillbrow. As we talked to the 30 or so people who started coming to meetings there, we began to realise how much need there was in this desperately poor area. The work grew and grew, and in April we registered a new charity, The Mission, and moved into an old war memorial building close to the railway station.

The Hillbrow area was one of the most densely populated in the country: once apartheid was dismantled, and South Africa's borders were more open, black Africans from other countries had come flooding in. Conditions might be poor in this overcrowded area of Johannesburg, but they were paradise compared with many other parts of Africa. South Africa had a first-world infrastructure, with schools, hospitals and jobs, but once you crossed the border you were back in the developing world. Illegal immigration was rife, and each new group of arrivals sought out their fellow countrymen for help and support. As a result, in Hillbrow there was a Nigerian sector, an Angolan sector, and groups from Mozambique, Senegal, Zimbabwe and so on. The black South Africans resented the incomers, while the usual lawless elements were busy making money from drugs, weapons and prostitution. The whole place was a tinderbox.

There was fierce competition for work, and terrible deprivation. We set out to bring practical help and hope to the destitute while sharing the love of Jesus. We set up work opportunities so that people could lift themselves out of poverty, and mostly we had great success. We did have one or two problems, where people succumbed to the temptation of making some easy money by selling the stock and equipment we had given them, and on one occasion the offenders were arrested and I had to go to court. The judge was surprised to hear that, before my appearance in the witness box, I had called at the cells to give some clothes to the man who stole from us. It was a witness of Christian forgiveness and care.

We remembered that prophecy in the Johannesburg bookshop: "God will use you mightily among the nations." We felt that God had given us a mandate to minister to all the African nations who had gathered there on our doorstep – and on the whole the people we met were willing to accept us. It was as though our work elsewhere in Africa entitled us to share with them: we were not whites who had never set foot outside our white South African enclaves; we had lived and worked in their countries. We wanted to bring salvation and hope into this dark, crime-infested situation, and people responded to our efforts. We spent a lot of time in prayer, and a lot of time arranging jobs and accommodation.

We are still involved with the work of The Mission, and raise money for it in the UK and South Africa. Our ultimate vision is to buy an accommodation building in Johannesburg where we can meet people's needs on the physical, emotional and spiritual levels: give them a home, work, guidance, help and pastoral care.

We also linked up with a South African lady who helped us to start The Mission Life Centre on a farm outside the city. There we helped boys who had been selling their bodies for sex on the streets of Johannesburg, and gave them work and a place to live. Teen World Outreach, an American organisation, sent thirteen students from the USA and Canada to work with us on a short-term outreach project, and they painted the farm buildings and shared in our ministry to the boys on the farm and in local shanty towns.

The day before they left, they visited a local school with gifts of sweets and beads, and they showed the children how to make a "salvation bracelet" with different-coloured beads, to help them remember the message of the gospel. They threaded the beads onto a string, telling them Bible verses as they went:

"The first knot reminds us that when we were born, God loved us and planned our lives (Psalm 139:13–16). The black bead stands for sin, which separates us from God (John 3:20,21). The red bead stands for the blood of Jesus, shed for us to pay for our sins (Romans 5:8). The white bead reminds us that we are forgiven when we accept Jesus as Lord (Acts 2:38). A blue bead stands for baptism, when we confess our faith (Romans 10:9–11). A gold bead shows that we will share Jesus' glory for ever (Revelation 21:1–3)."

Then they led the children in a prayer. Unfortunately, the Western team did not know much about tribal religions, and didn't realise that some of the African pupils thought they were encouraging them to wear a fetish bracelet and become Satan worshippers! Our students were threatened and assaulted, and the school principal came out to our farm to question us. It was a while before I was able to explain the meaning of the salvation bracelets, and that none of our workers was trying to cast a spell over the school students.

The new mission found plenty of work lying ready to its hand, and we were happy in the knowledge that we were preaching the gospel everywhere we went. Life in the new South Africa was still hard; crime rates were soaring, and many people were desperately poor. One winter morning a worker at The Mission asked me to help him look for a woman who had been coming to us for a few days. We found her lifeless body lying in the shrubs behind the building, covered with a cardboard box. She was huddled in a foetal position against the cold, only a few yards from a place where she could have found food and warmth. I felt helpless when I realised how many deaths like this there would be in the bitterly cold winter months, among the many who had no home, no money for food, and no hope.

There were other problems, too: when Tara had a road accident it was half an hour before an ambulance arrived. Fortunately she was OK, but some of the occupants of the other vehicle were injured, and as the ambulance was a private service the paramedics refused to treat them. It was two hours before a government ambulance came to collect them. It was horrifying to realise that in the new South Africa life was still easy if you were rich enough to afford medical insurance. If you relied on the state services you could be left to die at the side of the road.

The roads were very dangerous: two good friends of ours died in a head-on collision with a young drunk driver, and we were profoundly affected by their deaths. Richard Gibbs had come from the UK to attend Rhema Bible Training College, and he was one of the most gifted young men I knew – a trained teacher, able to speak three languages, skilled in working with computers, and shining with a love of people and a commitment to Jesus as his Lord. Tara and I had been present when he married his lovely wife, Sharon, and now they were gone from us, their lives wiped out in an instant. Seeing deaths like this made me all the more aware of how important it is that we should do God's will while we can: we never know how long we will have on this earth. It gave me a sense of urgency to do all I could to help others, and to walk in the will of God.

I took this feeling in prayer to the Lord, and he showed me that once again the old John had been trying to run the show. I was overseeing the work at The Mission, checking on the farm, visiting, preaching, teaching and running crusades. Every crusade was a huge undertaking, and I always put 110 per cent of effort into everything I did, returning home in a state of exhaustion each time. The stress of spending weeks away from my family, living and working in harsh and tiring conditions, was not good for any of us. I realised that I was running my chariot into the ground, and dragging my family behind me. We needed to catch our breath, and give our family time to establish a home and some security. Once again I began to pray that God would show us where he wanted us to be.

CHAPTER 17

Mission Link
International

IN THE YEAR 2000 Tara and I were invited by a friend of ours, Gerri Di Somma, to join him in the UK. He and his wife, Michelle, were both graduates of Rhema Bible Training College, and had been called by God to establish a church in Bristol, the Carmel Christian Centre. The work there was expanding, and he needed someone with experience to help in street evangelism. Tara and I prayed about it and we both felt that this was the next step we had to take in faith. Although we had spent ten months in the UK in 1996, we were still stepping into the unknown with no idea what awaited us and our children as we started a new life in England.

Gerri and Michelle established Carmel in 1996, meeting first in community halls and then in a warehouse before moving to the current address. Today the church has a congregation of around 350. Their vision was that the church should reach out and touch the local community, spiritually, emotionally and physically, preaching the kingdom of God and healing the sick. The Di Sommas also believed that the church should identify, train and support believers in whatever area of ministry God had called them to, and so they established the Anchor Bible Training Centre, which runs courses for Christian development.

We were accepted into the fellowship of the church and quickly began to feel at home. We had a small income from Tara's part-time work with a pension company, and I was paid for lecturing in Mission and Evangelism, but this was not enough to sustain us as a family. I did some plumbing to help our finances, but otherwise we trusted God for our needs. The local area is quite poor and unemployment is high, and many of our multicultural population are in great need, both materially and spiritually. I could see that my experience in street ministry would be useful as we started to reach out to people in the parks and shopping centres.

At the same time, we registered our charity, Mission Link International, combining our activities in Bristol with those in South Africa. We had left The Mission in the capable hands of Jacques Scharnik and his team, and they continue to feed and clothe between 700 and 1,000 people on the Johannesburg streets. We are also in partnership with Tracy Dudlu and her Agape inner-city project, where she cares for twelve abandoned children. Many of her "family" suffer from HIV/AIDS, which they have contracted from their mothers, who are mainly sex workers. With anti-retroviral drugs and good nutrition, Tracy has been able to sustain the precious lives of these children, when so many of their fellows have died on the city streets.

I still take part in ministry activities in Africa, and in May 2002 I was invited to minister at a week's outreach in Uganda, speaking at a pastors' conference during the day and at the gospel crusades at night. I was working with two other pastors – one from South Africa, the other from Bristol – and by the end of the week we had all seen the power of God moving among the leaders. They were filled with the Spirit and ready to go out and do great works for God. The evening crusades were also greatly blessed, though I'm sure most of the equipment was kept working mainly by the power of prayer. I had a look at the electrical systems and they seemed to consist of a muddle of wires held together with solder! I stood on a stage made from trees cut freshly from the forest, and thought how wonderful it was to be back in Africa, if only for eight days.

A year later, in May 2003, our second son, Dylan John, was born. I am so proud of my family – Jade, my little princess, and the miracle child who saved my life; Liam, my brave son with the heart of a lion who is so like me; and now Dylan, who is another blessing from the Lord. Most of all, I'm proud of my lovely wife, Tara, who is my rock. When we married, some of my friends looked at her fragile beauty and wondered if she was strong enough to endure living with me and my calling, but she has proved herself time and time again. She has endured tremendous hardships as we lived in tough conditions in the bush, and she has uprooted herself and come halfway across the world with me, and she still gives herself to the work we share and keeps our children secure and happy in their home. I am a man with many blessings to thank God for!

I still kept up my fitness training all this time: as part of a fund-raising effort for foreign students at the Bible school, in 2001 I completed a six-day cycle challenge in Jordan, and I ran the London Marathon in 2002, 2003 and 2004 – the last two times to raise funds for "Blankets for Africa". People in England find it difficult to believe that it gets cold in South Africa, but in the interior and the high veldt, temperatures plummet to minus double figures for three months of the year. People die of cold there, like the woman who died in the garden of The Mission in Johannesburg.

In July 2003 I collected a truck and trailer in Johannesburg and set off on yet another journey, like so many I had done over the years. This time I bought sweets and drinks to give to the children in the townships, and drove to Frankfort in Free State Province, a small farming town. I stayed with pastor Mike van Blerk of Kainos Worship Centre, and we visited local townships where we shared the message of Jesus Christ and handed out the blankets. It was wonderful to see the joy on people's faces as they wrapped the warm cloth around them, and to hear them joining in the songs of praise and thanksgiving. I was glad to see that the Afrikaans church had established a care clinic and an AIDS home, and was working with the African churches in the township – something that would never have happened in the old days. It seemed to me that in every place we stopped there was a funeral going on, and every one was an AIDS victim. In Qalabotjha Township I met some care workers who are helping grandparents who have been left to care for AIDS orphans, with no welfare system except their own small state pensions. I was beginning to understand the grip this terrible disease has on Africa.

Back in Bristol I carried on with the work we are doing to reach out to the local community in Knowle West, taking the gospel to the poor just as we do in Africa. People in Bristol are not barefoot or starving, thanks to the benefit system, but nevertheless there are hundreds of families who are living on the poverty line, with no hope of ever having more than the barest minimum to survive. We provide lots of activities for children who otherwise have nothing much to do with their spare time. At Christmas we ran a children's party, with Colin the Clown for entertainment, "Happy Meals" for refreshment, and presents for everyone. We also went out to the local estates, where we found lots of homes where parents couldn't afford to buy Christmas presents for their children, and they were so grateful when we knocked on the door with a box of gifts.

Our aim in Bristol is largely to act as a catalyst, helping the local churches to work together on short-term projects. We treat each event as a crusade, where we plan and prepare, run the event, make an impact and then withdraw. For instance, at Easter we organised a treasure hunt, with chocolate eggs to be collected, and a gospel message for the children and for the parents who brought them. The churches welcome this approach because we come in as "outsiders" – at our own expense – and provide a focus for them to work around. We are non-threatening because we are not a church in our own right, and so those who come to faith at these events are fed into the local churches. We are also able to provide a training ground for young people who have a heart for mission, showing them how to run similar events in their own communities.

I also visit the local Young Offenders' Institute, where I can talk to the young men and pray with them. Ministering to prisoners is very close to my heart, as I often feel that if things had gone differently in my life, and I hadn't found Jesus, I could so easily have ended up in prison myself. I do a lot of counselling, mainly with young men who have heard me speak. I think they recognise that I'm trustworthy, and that whatever they share with me is totally confidential before God. They also know that I'm unshockable: I've seen and heard most things over the years. The Holy Spirit makes me bold, and I'm not afraid to tell them straight how I see things – usually I see them shake a bit, and then they agree about what's going on in their lives, and I can help them to reach out to God for his help. My message is always the same: the love of God is powerful for forgiveness, and his grace will stir up his gifts in them, and enable them to do his will, and whatever work he has placed in their hearts. Not a day goes past without someone calling, asking me to be a listening ear. I'm fortunate that I have Tara at home, to counsel me in turn, and keep me grounded in my lovely family.

I always share the gospel wherever I am, whether I'm talking to the waitress or the bank clerk; I tell them that God loves them and wants them to know him. People (with their typical English reserve!) may think this is a brave thing to do, but what have I got to lose? I may never see them again. They never seem to be offended, perhaps because I have a friendly smile and a warm manner, and they can tell I really believe what I'm saying to them.

If I have a vision for the future, it is for China. I will never forget Africa, nor stop working hard to support the relief work there, especially for the AIDS orphanages and homes, but there are now many strong believers in Africa. The country is well served by people who can preach the gospel of God's love. I see a greater need for evangelism now in Europe and the USA, but most of all in China, where doors are beginning to open once more. I would love to run crusades there, and I believe that eventually God will make it possible for us to work there.

I never forget the promise that God made me in that Christian bookshop: that he would use me "mightily among the nations". The work I'm doing at the moment – raising funds for South Africa, and working with churches in Bristol – doesn't feel much like it. Yet I can see that foundations are being laid: we have set up Mission Link International; we have an office and some faithful Christian supporters. I believe that God will fulfil his will for us in his good time, if I can only learn patience. "My brethren, count it all joy when you fall into various trials, knowing that the testing of your faith produces patience. But let patience have its perfect work, that you may be perfect and complete, lacking nothing" (James 1:2-4, New King James Version).

I've kept in touch with several of my old comrades from Delta Company, especially Gungie and Dougie. Gungie has moved to the USA, and one day we were talking on the phone when he told me that he was still plagued by the bad dreams and horrific memories of our time in Angola. "Sometimes I hear voices," he confessed. "Do you think I'm going mad?"

I told him that he wouldn't go mad – I had been praying for him for many years, and God had him safely in his hand. I encouraged him to pray and ask Jesus into his life, because he is the only sure stronghold against all the evil in the world. Gungie did just that, and he is now a Christian. Last time we spoke he reminded me of the saying, "Old airborne soldiers never die – they just regroup in hell." "Well, we're going to regroup in heaven!" he said.

Dougie, too, has become a Christian. He lives in Jersey, making replica Mercedes Benz cars, but he still keeps his hand in by doing parachute jumps – he has "Jesus Saves" printed inside the canopy of his chute, so everyone sees it as he comes floating down! I've got a picture of the three of us in a helicopter all those years ago: when we were all in the army together, we never thought we would still be alive 25 years later, let alone all Christians. We three are a witness to God's transforming power.

So many of our old comrades have fallen victim to drink and drugs, still fleeing from their guilt and anger. I know from experience that you can run away as much as you like. You can join the French Foreign Legion from the age of 17 to the age of 40, and they'll give you a new name and a new life. But eventually you have to leave, and then you have to face up to who you really are and what you've really done. Back in South Africa, Archbishop Tutu set up the Truth and Reconciliation Commission, but I went to a better one – I went to Jesus. He made me a new creation; he gave me a new mind, a new body and a new understanding. He gave me a new calling – to love the people I used to hurt. There is nothing on earth as rewarding as doing the work God has prepared for you.

God the Father has now become my father. He cares for me and has my best interests at heart. My earthly father and I are reconciled. We have now reached a place where we can learn from and appreciate each other, and we go from strength to strength in our relationship. However difficult the first step, it is never too late to begin the journey of reconciliation.

When I give my testimony I tell people that I am not proud of the life I lived as a young man. If you have always been a Christian, and you don't have a dramatic testimony, be glad. It doesn't mean that you're soft, just that God placed his hand upon you early in your life. Anything is better than this tale of evil and violence, but I had to walk my own path before I could recognise the call of Jesus.

I learned about Jesus by meeting him, and I recognised that he was my saviour and my Lord. I don't tell people that their experience has to be like mine. Jesus meets people where they are, and your meeting with the shepherd may be different from mine. You can speak Elizabethan English to God if you want – he won't mind. It isn't my way; I like to speak to God in my own voice. You can go to church, but be aware that Christianity isn't lived in church – it's lived in the heart. You can be "religious", but God isn't – he's in everyday things, he's real, and he dances and rejoices over those who believe and come to him. He is a God of love and grace.

God has a plan for your life, and you can live in that vision, or you can turn your back on it: it's up to you. If this book has touched your heart, I ask you to pray this prayer with me:

> *Lord Jesus, I know I am a sinner and I need your forgiveness. Thank you for dying on the cross for me and offering me your gift of eternal life. I invite you into my heart to be my Saviour and Lord. Amen.*

If you have prayed this prayer, or would like me to contact you and pray with you, you can reach me by email on:

info@missionlinkinternational.com

or by writing to:

John Delaney
Mission Link International
PO Box 2214
Bristol
BS9 7HL.

Visit our website on:
www.johndelaney.com

Epilogue

WHEN I WAS 17 my greatest ambition was to be a ParaBat. I didn't think there could be anything in the world as exciting as being known as an elite soldier and facing death on the battlefield. For years after I had done my National Service I still thought that, because nothing in my experience came close to the exhilaration and adrenalin rush of jumping from an aircraft; it made me feel really alive.

Nowadays I know I was mistaken. I have found something even more exciting than living as a soldier of the South African Defence Force: living as a soldier for Christ. When Jesus took over my life, he gave me a better one. Now I don't want to hurt or kill anyone – I want to love them, care for them, rejoice with them.

God hasn't changed my personality; he accepts me as he made me, with all my energy and enthusiasm, just as I was as a child, before life turned some of it sour. I still make mistakes, of course, but there is one big difference. Now I know I am loved, redeemed, and forgiven. God has placed his calling on my life, to tell people about Jesus.

The discipline of the army changes you; it teaches you new priorities, and the only similar discipline I know is Christianity, for turning your life around. The Bats never left a man behind – I remember seeing a man jump on a wounded friend and shield him with his body. When I asked him afterwards why he did it, he said, "He'd taken one shot and he couldn't afford to take another." He couldn't let his friend die. As Christians we have the same responsibility. We can't let our friends go on into danger and despair, when we can offer them the gifts of security and hope and salvation. We have to love one another as Christ has loved us.

Now my greatest ambition is to work for Jesus Christ, to be a soldier for him, fighting against the fear, the injustice, the poverty and the sorrow that are the enemies of mankind. The challenges of that life – and the rewards of seeing people meet with Jesus and accept him as their saviour – are all the excitement I need.